CW00657736

PRACTICAL Art SCHOOL

OIL PAINTING

OIL PAINTING

GERALD WOODS

OIL PAINTING

A Little, Brown Book

Designed, written and edited by
The Bridgewater Book Company Ltd

First published in Great Britain in 1996
by Little, Brown and Company

CLB 4080
© 1995 Colour Library Books Ltd
Godalming, Surrey
The moral right of the author has been asserted.

All rights reserved. No part of this publication may be reproduced, stored in a retrieval system,
or transmitted, in any form or by any means, without the prior permission in writing of the publisher,
nor be otherwise circulated in any form of binding or cover other than that in which it is published and
without a similar condition including this condition being imposed on the subsequent purchaser.

A CIP catalogue record for this book
is available from the British Library

ISBN 0 316 91330 8

10 9 8 7 6 5 4 3 2 1

Designed by Peter Bridgewater / Annie Moss
Edited by Viv Croot
Managing Editor Anna Clarkson
Photography by Zul Mukhida
Typesetting by Kirsty Wall

Colour separation by Scantrans PTE Ltd, Singapore
Printed and bound in Spain by Graficas Estella

Little, Brown and Company (UK)
Brettenham House
Lancaster Place
London WC2E 7EN

Contents

At-A-Glance Guide

Introduction

I am always fascinated by those television programmes which feature a well-known cook or chef, demonstrating the various stages in producing a gastronomic delight according to a prescribed recipe. Having assembled all the ingredients together, they blend and mix them together with a deftness and panache that can only come from years of experience.

The English artist Walter Richard Sickert (1860–1942) once said that painting was a bit like cooking: once you've got the ingredients right, the actual cooking of the dish is not too difficult. Continuing the analogy, he also advised that oil paints should be mixed to the consistency of soft butter. This book, like most books concerned with painting techniques, is essentially a recipe book. I would, therefore, consider it as a mark of success if, in a year or so, I were to discover a copy covered in accretions of paint!

The first two sections of the book are concerned with materials, techniques, media and ways of handling them. The handling of a medium is, of course, personal to the artist and his or her work is often recognised by distinctive brushmarks. The better informed you are about technique, the more confident you feel in executing the finished painting – the cook who mixes the ingredients too tentatively, produces a dish that is less than appetising! The preliminary exercises in mixing and using colour are, therefore, a necessary prerequisite to making paintings which look as though they have been produced with ease. Giorgio Vasari (1511–1571) puts it more eloquently when he says, 'The work should attain perfection without any appearance of effort, without the spectator feeling any of the pangs suffered by the painter making it.'

The main aim of this book is to demonstrate ways of producing oil paintings which are personal inasmuch as they are part of the way you really see life. We tend often to forget that the artist never paints things as they are, but as he or she sees them.

The project section of the book is invaluable in that it demonstrates how three artists, working from the same subjects, interpret what they have seen individually – often producing paintings which are strikingly different in style and use of colour and tone – even though they have shared the same source of reference.

The critique of each project highlights both positive and negative aspects of each painting, and also illustrates how each artist is able to deal better with some subjects than others.

Finally, I hope that by their example the reader will feel sufficiently encouraged to begin painting – inevitably some attempts will end in failure, but often the process of failure itself leads to new discoveries and new forms of expression.

MATERIALS AND TECHNIQUES

The Studio

The word 'studio' has all kinds of romantic associations. The French word 'atelier' which means workshop is probably more relevant. Most artists, however, have to make use of whatever space is available – which might not be much more than the kitchen table! It is, however, always fascinating to see an artist's place of work; Alexander Liberman's book, *The Artist in his Studio* (1960) offers a unique insight into the studios of such artists as Renoir, Bonnard, Matisse, Braque and many others.

In Braque's studio in Varengeville, Normandy, for example, the immense room was completely cut off from the outside world. Instead of clear panes of glass, the windows were opaque. Everything was ordered and spaces divided according to their function. Sources of inspiration included objects found on the nearby beach – pebbles, pieces of driftwood, starfish and bleached bones. The walls were covered with paper cut-outs, Indian rugs, Polynesian shields and Etruscan sculpture. Brushes and pencils were laid out in order on slats of corrugated cardboard, oil cans served for mixing colour, and palettes were attached to a tree-trunk fixed to the floor with iron supports.

Don't be deterred by lack of space – a vast studio is only necessary if you intend producing paintings on a very large scale. Diffused light is ideal for oil painting and is easy to achieve. Simply cover the lower part of the window in your studio with tissue paper taped to the frame.

You will obviously need a good solid working table for stretching canvas and priming. Additionally, you might prefer a painting table to a hand-held palette. You will need storage space for materials and, if space allows, a rack for finished canvases and frames. A plan chest is very useful for storing drawings to keep them flat. Other painting materials can also be stored in it.

A well ordered studio with everything in its space and divided according to function. The venetian blinds provide diffused light, which is ideal for oil painting.

GENERAL
STUDIO EQUIPMENT

1 Charcoal
2 Hammer
3 Canvas tacks
4 Staple gun
5 Masking tape
6 Scissors
7 Cutting tools
8 Steel rule
9 T-square
10 Rags
11 Broad house-painter's brush
12 Glass jars and old tins for paint and media

Canvas and Other Supports

14 A support is the name given to the various supporting surfaces on which all oil paintings are carried out. The primary function of a support is to provide a stable, and solid surface which will readily receive whatever technique or medium you intend using. Wood panels, stretched canvas, hardboard (masonite), canvas board, compressed fibre board, cardboard and metal are all supports.

When considering which type of support would be most suitable for your own purposes, focus on factors such as weight, size and cost, as well as surface qualities of different kinds of material.

WOOD PANELS

Historically these are the oldest type of support, though they were largely replaced by stretched canvas during the Renaissance. Many varieties of wood are suitable; however, hard woods such as mahogany are more stable than softer woods which are liable to warp.

All wood panels should be cut from well-seasoned wood and free from cracks or knots. Thin panels can be given additional strength by screwing batoning to the reverse side. If well-seasoned wood is difficult to obtain, you could salvage old furniture, particularly door panels.

The weight of a large wooden panel could prove to be a problem for the landscape painter, though small panels are eminently suitable for painting directly from nature.

HARDBOARD

Hardboard (or masonite) is mid-brown or dark brown in colour and is made from wood-pulp compressed into thin sheets. This type of board is perhaps the most widely used support for oil painting, because it is inexpensive, lightweight and strong. Many people make the mistake of using the textured side of the board, probably because it is akin to the texture of canvas. The some-

Supports for oil painting includes, from top to bottom, stretched linen canvas, canvas board, cardboard, hardboard, and sanded plywood.

what mechanical 'tooth' is very pronounced, however, and will dominate the painting unless a thick impasto is applied. The smooth side is preferable, but should be sanded slightly to make the surface more receptive to primer.

PAPER AND CARD

Rembrandt, Delacroix and Cézanne all occasionally used paper as a support for oil painting. A good quality rough surface watercolour paper is ideal and can be given additional stability by being stuck down on to board. A thin coating of gesso primer painted on both sides of the paper will counteract its absorbency. One note of caution is that unsized and unprimed cardboard tends to attract fungus and mildew unless stored in dry conditions or framed and sealed behind glass.

OIL SKETCHING PAPER

This is a commercially produced paper which comes ready primed and has a canvas-like texture. It is useful for landscape and figure studies, though some people are put off by the rather mechanical texture of the surface.

CANVAS

This is the traditional support for oil painting and the one most favoured by professional artists. Fine and coarse weaves of cloth offer a variety of surfaces. The characteristic 'tooth' of the canvas is, when primed, particularly responsive to oil paint.

A stretched canvas is light and easy to transport and can, if necessary, be taken off the stretcher and rolled up for storage.

The finest canvas is made from linen which has a fine weave and is less liable to shrink or stretch than other materials. Cotton canvas is more economical but is generally softer and more prone to distortion. A professionally prepared cotton canvas, however, is adequate for most purposes and less expensive than linen.

STRETCHING A CANVAS

The drum-like tautness of canvas is achieved by stretching it over a wooden frame called a stretcher. If you are a skilled woodworker and have adequate mitring equipment, you may prefer to make your own stretchers. The mitred corners of each length must be slotted and the edges bevelled so that they do not press against the stretched canvas. Ready-made stretcher pieces can be bought in standard sizes and very quickly put together.

1 *Cut the canvas with an overlap of 50mm all round the assembled stretcher. Make sure that the stretcher is completely square, and that all the bevels are on the same side.*

2 *Tack the centre of one side firmly in position with a tack hammer. You could also use a staple gun if preferred.*

3 *Stretch the canvas taut and tack the opposite side in the centre. Continue working in this way from one side to the other and left and right of the centre.*

4 *Fold the remaining flaps neatly over at each corner of the stretcher as shown above.*

5 *Tack down each corner. Finally, knock the wooden wedges (which are supplied with stretchers) into the gaps on each mitre, two to each corner.*

Hardboard can be primed with gesso primer. The first coat will normally dry in 30 minutes. A second and third coat can be applied after finely sanding the surface slightly at each stage.

Priming

As its name suggests, primer is the first coating of paint applied to the support. Apart from providing a ground on which to paint, the main function of a primer is to prevent the colour from sinking into the support. If, for instance, one were to paint directly onto an unprimed canvas, the oil which binds the pigment would be rapidly absorbed, leaving a residue of colour which is difficult to control with a brush. Oil paint has a tendency to darken with age but a coat of white primer will help to ensure that the tone and brilliance of the colour is retained.

SIZING

Before the canvas or support is primed it should be given a coating of size. The best size is made from rabbit-skin glue, available in crystal form from artists' materials shops. The sheets of glue or crystals should be dissolved in warm water and stirred until liquid. (When cold it should be the consistency of soft jelly.) The size is applied while still warm and allowed to dry thoroughly before priming. To prevent the canvas from sticking to the stretcher, insert pieces of card during the drying process. Some artists prefer to use the natural colour of the cloth as a ground for painting and do not therefore add a coat of primer.

Hardboard and other water-resistant materials do not generally need to be sized before priming.

WHICH PRIMER?

Traditionally, the main priming pigment for oil painting is white lead to which glue size and boiled linseed oil is added. The toxic nature of white lead, however, has proved to be a health risk, Titanium White or Zinc White are generally used now.

The introduction of ready-mixed acrylic grounds has made life easier for those artists who do not wish to spend a lot of time on preparation. Acrylic gesso dries rapidly and provides a fine matt white surface which is very receptive to brush marks.

If you are applying two or three coats of primer to your support, allow each coat to dry thoroughly and sandpaper any uneven patches. Gesso primer can be given a final polish with a damp rag.

MAKING PRIMER

If you prefer to make your own primer, the following recipe might prove useful:

Mix equal quantities of chalk whiting powder and Titanium White together with five parts rabbit-skin glue and one part linseed oil. Blend the powders together on a glass slab with a palette knife, leaving a depression in the middle. Pour in half of the glue while it is still warm, then the oil, and followed with the rest of the glue. Mix to the consistency of double cream. Dilute this paste further with a little hot water and brush directly onto the canvas. This will produce a ground which is slightly porous. If desired, the surface can be sealed with a weak solution of gelatine and water, to which a touch of Titanium White has been added.

A number of alternative recipes for primers will be found in standard textbooks, such as those by Hiler and Mayer available in art supply shops.

LINSEED OIL

RABBITSKIN GLUE

CHALK WHITING POWDER

WINSOR & NEWTON
Artists'
Oil Colour
Titanium
White

644
Permanence AA
Series 1

Blanc de Titane
Titanweiss
Blanco de Titanio
Bianco di titanio

37 ml e
1.25 U.S.fl.oz.

Brushes and Painting Knives

I have known painters whose attachment to their brushes borders on the superstitious! There is the feeling that, if a particular brush has served one well, it would be tempting providence to replace it with another. In my experience, a brush needs to be 'broken-in' by regular use before it will render exactly the marks I want to make. Sable brushes improve with age if they are cleaned properly after use.

The best brushes are still handmade and it is really a false economy to buy cheaper mass-produced brushes. Brushes used for oil painting are made from hog's hair and sable. Additionally, there are an increasing number of brushes made from synthetic materials such as nylon. A good-quality brush will hold its shape when paint is applied to the canvas. The bristles should be neither too limp nor too springy but should respond sensitively to the direct action of mark-making.

Oil painting brushes have a wooden handle about 30cm/12 inches long. In terms of size of the brush head, No. 1 is the finest and 12/14 the broadest.

Hog's hair brushes are made in three main shapes. Flat brushes have a wedge-shaped square tip. They are used mainly for blocking in large areas of colour, particularly in the first stages of a painting. Round brushes taper towards the tip and are used for more linear brush strokes. The filbert shape, which actually resembles the rounded tip of a finger, is also used to apply colour broadly. Sable or 'soft' brushes are used primarily for finer detail. They are also manufactured as flats, rounds and filberts.

No. 11 hog's hair round brush.

Painting knives with thin flexible steel blades.

No. 10 hog's hair
long flat brush.

No. 6 hog's hair short flat brush.

No. 9 hog's hair
short filbert.

No. 3 hog's hair short flat brush.

No. 8 pure sable brush.

No. 10 round
sable brush.

CLEANING BRUSHES

Cleaning your brushes and palette should become a ritual after each painting session. I find it particularly satisfying (even if the day's work has gone badly) to clean and prepare everything so that I can start afresh the next day.

The brushes should be first rinsed in turpentine substitute or petrol and carefully wiped on a soft rag. Each brush is then degreased by activating the bristles in washing-up detergent cupped in the palm of one's hand. Rinse the brush thoroughly in warm water, squeeze out excess water and re-shape the bristles with thumb and forefinger.

PAINTING KNIVES

These flexible knives are either flat or trowel-shaped and are also known as palette knives.

They are mainly useful for mixing and blending colour on a palette or painting table. Moreover, they are particularly useful for scraping out or scraping back unwanted passages in a painting.

Although some artists use a knife as a painting instrument, my own feeling is that a knife is not as sensitive as a brush and I do not much like the smooth slabs of paint it deposits on the canvas or board. Having said that, however, there are some fine passages of 'knife-work' in the landscape paintings of Turner and Constable.

Easels

20

It is perfectly possible to work on oil paintings without an easel; indeed, some artists prefer working in a less formal way on an old table. Nevertheless, for the professional artist or serious amateur, a studio easel is a worthwhile investment. A well-made studio easel will hold your canvas or board in a rigid position, the height can be adjusted for a standing or sitting position, and the easel can be moved to any position to catch the best light.

A studio easel is usually constructed from a rigid H-shaped vertical frame set into a base which is moved on castors. The canvas rests on a shelf which sometimes incorporates a compartment for brushes and colours. A sliding block holds the canvas firmly in position at the top.

The canvas is moved up and down by means of an adjustable ratchet which may also be tilted backwards or forwards from the vertical to give greater flexibility. Some easels adjust so that the canvas can lie horizontal for watercolour work.

RADIAL EASELS

This is the type of easel most commonly used in art schools, especially in the life-painting studio. The upright column is held by a large locking wing-nut connected to three short tripod legs. By loosening the wing-nut, the column can be tilted backwards or forwards. The canvas rests on an adjustable shelf, and is held at the top by a sliding block.

SKETCHING EASELS

These folding easels are made primarily for landscape painting. They combine lightness, strength and simplicity. Made either from beechwood or a lightweight metal such as aluminium, they can accommodate a canvas height of 863mm/34 inches. There is no reason why this type of easel should not also be used in the studio, providing that the spiked tripod legs are supported by blocks or an old carpet or rug.

LEFT *Studio easels. The self-assembly easel (far left) has an adjustable lower shelf. The beechwood radial easel (centre) tilts to provide different working positions. The tilting radial easel (right) has a central pivotal joint so the canvas can be fixed in any position.*
RIGHT *Sketching easels. The lightweight beechwood easel (right) can be tilted to any angle. A more robust version is shown in the centre. Two lightweight metal folding easels (far left) with telescopic legs.*

Photographs courtesy of Winsor & Newton

Palettes

The kidney-shaped wooden palette has become a kind of professional symbol for the oil painter. Strangely enough, very few painters in my experience actually use the traditional wooden palette for mixing their colour – most prefer to use a glass slab or sheet of plastic on a painting table. Much depends on the kind of painting you are doing. The concentration needed for portrait painting, for instance, might be unduly disturbed by constantly having to turn away from the model to mix colour on a table, whereas a palette enables the artist to have all the colours he or she is using readily at hand.

Wooden palettes are usually made from mahogany. The weight of the palette is critical, since it should be comfortable to hold for hours at a time. The oval thumb hole should be sanded so that it does not cut into the skin. Containers known as 'dippers' can be clipped onto the edge of the palette for oil, turpentine or varnish. Oblong wooden palettes will fit more readily into a painting box. White plastic palettes make it somewhat easier to judge colour values, especially when working on a white canvas, but the surface is less sympathetic to work on than wood. Expendable parchment palettes, which are produced as tear-off pads of 50 sheets, are convenient since you can simply dispose of unwanted colour at the end of each painting session – although you may waste quite a lot of paint this way.

This selection of palettes includes birch plywood, throwaway vegetable parchment, traditonal curved mahogany and chinaware (for glazes).

Paint Additives

All oil paints produced in tubes contain a certain amount of linseed or poppy oil and you need to consider this before further dilution. There are painters who prefer to use oil colours straight out of the tube thus retaining the essential richness of the coloured pigment. In practice, however, most painters discover that they need to reduce the consistency of oil paint in order to achieve full expression in the character of individual brushmarks.

There is a general rule that you should work from thin to fat, though some artists enjoy working in a thick impasto throughout.

There are mainly three ways of reducing the consistency of oil paint: with more oil, with varnish, or with an evaporative essence such as petrol or turpentine. The most common painting medium is a mixture of distilled turpentine and linseed oil.

For those who, like myself, are allergic to turpentine, oil of spike lavender (available from artists' materials shops) is a suitable alternative – but it is slower to dry.

WHITE SPIRIT

Sometimes known as turpentine substitute, this tends to dull the colour, and should be used mainly for cleaning purposes.

LINSEED AND POPPY OIL

This strong and reliable medium is chemically processed in different ways. **Cold pressed linseed oil** is a slightly yellow oil which is extracted without heat. It increases gloss and transparency while reducing the pigment. **Stand oil** (prepared by heating linseed oil or drying it in the sun) is a pale, viscous oil that will retard drying and improve colour flow when used in conjunction with turpentine. **Drying linseed oil** is of a darker colour and will increase the drying rate of oil colours. **Sun-bleached poppy oil** is a pale, non-yellowing oil which is useful when painting with whites and pale yellows.

There are numerous commercially formulated painting media, many of which are excellent. As a general rule, however, it is best to use only those which provide some indication of the ingredients used in their manufacture.

VARNISH

Varnishes are either used with other media as part of the painting process, or as a protective film for the finished painting. **Copal Varnish** has been used for many years with oil as a painting medium. It is highly viscous and difficult to handle – it also has a tendency to darken. **Damar Varnish** is a spirit-based varnish made from the resin of the Damar fir tree dissolved in turpentine. It can be used as a final varnish for the completed painting, producing a wax-like sheen rather than a high gloss. It can also be added to oil and turpentine to produce a painting medium which enriches the colour. **Mastic** is yellowish in colour, and has the advantage of drying quickly to produce a high gloss finish. It tends to darken with age and is subject to blooming.

The whole point of giving a painting a final coat of varnish is to protect it from dirt and discoloration. If in turn the varnish becomes dirty, it can be removed with alcohol and the painting re-varnished. This is a slightly risky process, however, since some of the paint might also be removed – especially if varnish has also been used as part of the painting medium.

A coat of varnish will not enhance a bad painting and might easily spoil a good one.

Before applying varnish, make sure that the pigment in the painting is really hard and free from moisture. The temperature should be even and the room free from dust.

Warm the painted surface first, using a hair-dryer or fan heater. Lay the board or canvas on a flat surface. Pour enough varnish into a dish to cover the whole painting. Using a broad, soft brush, apply the varnish lightly and rapidly under a good light.

A CAUTIONARY NOTE

Observe the correct drying times for all media and varnish.

Linseed oil can take from three to four days to dry, stand oil up to eight days, mastic and copal thirty-six hours.

Oil Paints

Coloured pigments from which oil paints are made are either mineral or organic in origin. Among the natural pigments are the earth colours: yellow, Yellow Ochre, Terre Verte and Ultramarine. Organic animal and vegetable pigments include Carmine, Sepia, the Madders (from the plant of that name) Gamboge, Indigo and Sap Green.

Artificial chemical compounds are the basis for other colours such as, Prussian Blue, Cobalt Blue and Viridian.

Oil paint is made from finely ground pigment held in a binding medium (oil) which enables it to be spread evenly and adhere to a prepared surface. The oil which binds the pigment does not evaporate but reacts to oxygen in the air and, as it dries slowly, it becomes a solid linoxyn. It is only when the oil and pigment are bound together in liquid form that they are soluble. Today, oil paints are sold in air-tight tubes and if you leave the screw-cap off for any length of time, you will find that the paint will solidify inside the tube. Before the introduction of collapsible tubes, artists had to grind colours afresh for each painting session.

In the manufacture of oil paint there are two basic operations. The raw lumps of pigment must be refined into individual particles and then dispersed in the liquid medium (linseed oil). Large mixing machines known as triple rolling mills are used for the dispersion process. Most colours will pass through the mill several times before they achieve the correct colour.

CHOOSING COLOURS

Some colours such as Ultramarine, are still hand-ground on a granite slab with a cone-shaped block of marble or glass called a muller. There are a number of factors to be taken into consideration when choosing colours – the suitability of the

colour itself for your purposes, the body, density, speed of drying and the degree of permanence.

Most artists have a predilection for certain colours, – whether it be a special colour such as Carmine, or Naples Yellow, or a range of colours of the same hue. The landscape painter might use an entirely different range of colours from someone who paints seascapes or portraits. For most purposes however, a basic range of ten to twelve colours will do. Titian, one of the greatest colourists, is said to have observed that a painter needs only three colours in his palette!

Technical analysis of Constable's palette at the Tate Gallery in London shows that he used Vermilion, Emerald Green, Chrome Yellow and Madder. Further examination of his painting of Flatford Mill reveals that he also used Prussian Blue, Yellow Ochre, Raw and Burnt Sienna.

Artists' colourmen of repute now provide information in their catalogues concerning the ingredients of their oil paints, as well as the degree of permanence of each colour.

WHITES

All the whites are dense and will give added density to transparent colours. Titanium White is used both as a primer and as a painting pigment. Flake White is made from white lead and is suitable for building up an impasto. Zinc White is fairly intense but is subject to cracking when dry.

Traditionally oil paint was freshly mixed for each painting session.

Most artists lay their palette out in the same order every time they paint so they can find the colours easily even when absorbed in their work.

BLUES

Cobalt – a clear mid-blue – tends to look transparent even when applied thickly. Cerulean Blue, a greener blue, is dense and very opaque. Ultramarine is a brilliant, slightly red/blue; it is semi-transparent and should be used with care in relation to other colours. Prussian Blue has a powerful green/blue stain which is very intense. Monastral Blue is a more recent transparent blue which is permanent and less cold than Prussian Blue.

GREENS

Viridian and Terre Verte are transparent greens – the latter was often used for underpainting by the Old Masters. Cadmium Green is a blend of Cadmium Yellow and Viridian. Cobalt Green is an opaque blue-green pigment; it is weak, with poor tinting strength. Emerald Green is useful for strong opaque tints; it turns black when used with Cadmium Yellow or Vermilion.

BROWNS AND BLACKS

Raw Sienna, which is sometimes considered to be a yellow, is transparent. Burnt Sienna is a red-brown which is permanent. Raw and Burnt Umber are both earth colours – the first is cool, the second warm.

Ivory Black is the most commonly used black, it is very intense and opaque. Lamp Black is slower to dry, but warmer in tone than ivory black.

VIOLETS

Cobalt Violet is a transparent colour that does not have very much covering power. Ultramarine Violet is a mid-tone with a tinge of blue.

YELLOWS

Lemon Yellow is a pale, transparent yellow that has a tinge of green. Chrome Yellow is an opaque yellow with a good covering power. It is supplied in different tones – Chrome Yellow Deep and Chrome Yellow Light. It is not permanent and is poisonous. Cadmium Yellow is more permanent and again is produced in different tones. Indian Yellow is a brilliant transparent yellow. Naples Yellow is opaque, being a blend of Cadmium White, red, and Yellow Ochre.

REDS

Cadmium Reds range in colour from a bright yellowish red to a deep red tinged with blue. They have a good degree of permanence and excellent covering power. Alizarin Crimson is an intense red with a hint of crimson – used in low concentrations it can become fugitive. Vermilion is a brilliant, very opaque red. Madder is a delicate crimson colour which is used mainly as a tint for other colours. Indian Red has a purple-brown tone – it is opaque with a good covering power. Venetian Red is a rich, dark red; it is opaque and permanent. Carmine is a very pure, transparent pinkish red, but is less permanent than other reds.

Modern oil paints are sold in air-tight metal tubes

Brush Techniques

The first marks made on the canvas are as important as the last – there is little point in trying to finish a painting that has started badly or with the wrong intentions. Delacroix felt that the first marks on canvas revealed everything that was essentially significant to the rest of the painting. 'The life of the work', he said, 'is already to be seen everywhere, and nothing in the development of this theme, in appearance so vague, will depart in the least from the artist's conception: it has scarcely opened to the light, and already it is complete.'

The work of a painter is often distinguished by the character of the brushstrokes made on the painting surface. We call this the 'handling' of the medium; that part which is most personal to the actual execution of the work. Van Gogh's paintings, for example, are characterised by his use of thick, expressive strokes, which stand in relief on the surface of the canvas. When we look at a painting by Degas, however, we are more conscious of the quality of the drawn line, particularly in his figure studies.

There is no one method of painting which can be described as the 'right' way – the importance lies with the product, not with the method of production. There are, however, ways of handling materials which ought to be explored and practised by any artist seriously intent on finding a personal means of expression through the medium of oil painting.

The novice painter starts with high expectations and is all too often put off by early failure. Think about what happens when, having bought all the necessary materials, you tackle the first painting – say a still life. The wedges of colour are squeezed out onto the palette looking fresh and untested; a hog's hair brush is dipped into the oil medium, and the coarse bristles take up a little colour; the first brushstrokes are made in response to the subject – but the paint isn't behaving as expected – there seems to be a disconnection between what was intended and the quality of the marks which actually appear on the canvas. When things go wrong technically, the concentration tends to go adrift. What usually happens is that you go on hoping that something significant will emerge from the layers of pigment which begin to accrue on the canvas. But by this time, you are no longer in control and things might get considerably worse before they get

better. Of course, the difficulties encountered should be seen in a positive light, rather than as a cause of despair. A lack of confidence in handling techniques can be remedied to some extent by a process of familiarisation through simple exercises.

First of all, you will need to learn how to control your brushes. If you have ever witnessed a signwriter at work (a rare sight these days!) you will have noticed how the hand moves slowly, but at a constant speed, to follow the curvature of the letterforms. It is a kind of swift, pivotal action from the wrist, which can be practised by painting spirals and full circles.

Using different actions and different types of brush you will be able to produce a rich variety of brushmarks and textures – from thin transparent glazes to a dry impasto. For the following exercises, you can use primed hardboard or even cardboard.

USING A MAHL STICK

A mahl stick is useful as a means of support for the painting hand when adding fine detail to a painting. It allows you to get close

OPPOSITE *A ruler can be used as a brush guide for making straight lines.*

RIGHT *A long hog's hair flat brush is used to practise the pivotal wrist action that helps good brush control.*

BELOW *Scumbling colour with a broad housepainter's brush.*

FAR RIGHT *Scumbled colour is used to evoke the effect of a storm-lashed coast in this seascape.*

to the painting without smudging it. A piece of ash dowel or bamboo has one end covered with a ball-shaped pad of chamois leather which rests on the canvas, while the end of the dowel or bamboo is supported by the free hand.

DRAWING STRAIGHT LINES

A decorator's yard-stick or metre stick is useful as an aid to drawing uprights and horizontals – particularly in architectural subjects. The loaded brush can be run along the edge of the stick as it is held about a centimetre from the surface.

SCUMBLING

The scumbling technique involves dragging one dry, opaque layer of paint lightly over another layer of a different colour, in such a way that parts of the first layer are still visible through the broken texture of the scumbling. This kind of irregular and unpredictable texture can be seen in the work of many artists, from Turner to Bonnard. The paint to be scumbled should be brushed out on the palette first until almost dry. Since the bristles of the

ABOVE *A hog's hair flat brush is used to produce a brushstroke which bears the imprint of the brush shape.*

brush tend to be splayed out of shape during this process, it is advisable to use a hog's hair brush, rather than a sable which might easily be damaged. The more pronounced the 'tooth' of the canvas, the better the effect of scumbling will be.

IMPASTO

When paint is so thick that it stands in low-relief bearing the imprint of the brush that has been used, it is 'impastoed'. Thick, solid areas of paint are sometimes found under glazes in work by Rembrandt, Turner, Courbet and others. The paint is best applied without much medium being added. It can be scraped back while still wet and re-worked if necessary.

GLAZING AND STAINING

Glazing is the process of applying transparent layers of oil paint over a solid colour, so that the colour and tone is distinctly

LEFT *In this seascape detail a heavy impasto has been laid with a painting knife to suggest the layered formation of advancing waves.*
RIGHT *A broad filbert brush is used to produce a bold impasto.*

modified. If, for example, a transparent glaze of Carmine Red were to be brushed over Ultramarine, it would produce a rich purple colour. Much depends on the thickness of the glaze and the intensity of the pigment in the solid colour.

When working on a white ground, the glazes can be built up like watercolour. But few artists work entirely in oil glazes since each coat of paint must be dry before applying the next. Glazes are best used in conjunction with other techniques such as under-painting, scumbling and impasto.

Some artists like to stain parts of the canvas with a wash of dilute colour, in contrast to passages in the same painting which are built up with impasto. It is a matter for experiment to determine the right approach for your own painting.

ABOVE *In this mixed-media painting of a Spanish church, dilute oil paint has been stained over the drawn detail with a soft rag to produce a transparent film of colour.*

LEFT *The rich colours of rusting plate iron on a freight wagon provided the inspiration for this painting, which combines collage with broad brush-strokes of 'dry' colour.*

BELOW *A medium filbert is used to produce a dilute stain of colour.*

Underpainting and Underdrawing

Underpainting is the preliminary drawing made in a single colour directly onto the canvas or board. All the fundamental problems of drawing, composition and tone are sorted out at this stage, leaving the artist free to deal with colour values.

It is, of course, perfectly possible to begin working without any kind of underdrawing or underpainting – given that you have a good sense of design, you could start working right away in terms of colour masses and tonal contrast. Much depends on the kind of subject you are painting. If, for instance, you are confronted by a coastal scene or landscape, where everything is distributed in terms of simple interlocking shapes, then it might make sense to begin working in blocks of colour, and to leave any finer delineation that may be necessary to a later stage in the development of the painting. If on the other hand, you are dealing with a subject of greater complexity, you might feel more confident by starting with an underdrawing or an underpainting.

From my own experience, I find it useful to have some kind of underlying framework or 'scaffolding' to build on. Additionally, corrections can easily be made during the early stages. The underlying linear structure of a painting can be carried out on a primed support with a soft pencil or charcoal. Such a drawing, however, will not be an integral part of the finished painting, since it will be cancelled out by the first layer of paint.

UNDERDRAWING WITH CHARCOAL

Working with charcoal allows a complete gestural freedom and the broad character of the medium prevents you from becoming too absorbed in fine detail. Corrections can be made by simply

LEFT *This lively under-painting harnesses all the vital elements of the composition together. The successful development of the painting will depend on the balance of colour and tone.*

OPPOSITE, RIGHT *Drawing of Zanora Cathedral, Spain in pencil made from direct observation.*

OPPOSITE, FAR RIGHT *The drawing is used as reference to produce an underpainting in dilute Burnt Sienna on canvas paper.*

wiping the pigment with a soft rag or finger. Excessive pigment can be removed by tapping the support. It is advisable to fix the drawing before painting. Not only will the charcoal make dirty a pale colour, but it is also disconcerting to work on top of a drawing which is unstable.

'I have now reached the point at which I have decided no longer to begin a painting with a charcoal sketch. It leads to nothing; one should attack a drawing directly with colour in order to draw well.' Vincent van Gogh, in a letter to his brother Theo, September, 1888.

UNDERPAINTING WITH A BRUSH

Many artists much prefer to start working with a brush. The paint is normally a thin glaze of a neutral colour such as Sepia, Ochre or pale blue. If you intend working over the underpainting with further glazes, then the underpainting should be applied more thickly. Van Eyck always started with an underpainting as a thin wash of colour, whereas Titian and Veronese did their underpaintings with thick pigment before overpainting with glazes.

For my own part, I find that often the first half-hour spent on an underpainting is the most satisfying aspect of the whole procedure. It is at this stage when everything is open and nothing is resolved, that I am most optimistic! I usually produce the underpainting with oil paint thinned with turpentine substitute.

If you are working on the coloured ground of a previously stained canvas, it is as well to lay-in the underpainting in a darker strength of the colour used for staining. I always try to produce paintings where part of the underpainting is exposed in the final painting – the alternation of transparency with opacity is, to my mind, one of the most interesting qualities of the medium. It is impossible, for example, to look at a painting by Degas, without being aware of the fact that the underpainting is an integral part of the finished painting.

The Venetians produced underpaintings in a range of warm and cool colours, to establish all the undertones before beginning the final painting. French eighteenth-century painters used a technique known as *grisaille*, a kind of monochromatic underpainting in tones of grey which shows through as a middle tone.

Painting Alla Prima

Alla Prima comes from the Italian, meaning 'at first'. When we talk of a painting that has been produced *alla prima*, we are describing the technique of completing the picture in one session. This method of painting has been popular since the nineteenth century and coincided with the fashion for painters to venture out of the studio to paint directly from nature.

It is a way of working which reached its apotheosis with the French Impressionists, who made it a basic tenet of their painting philosophy. There may be a number of practical reasons why a

RIGHT *This small portrait was painted in one short sitting of about an hour.* BELOW *Life study produced in a single sitting of two hours. The painting technique combines washes of oil paint with a heavier impasto.* FAR RIGHT *This garden scene was hurriedly painted between showers of rain in about three hours.*

painting must be completed in one session – the model sitting for a portrait may not be available for a second sitting, or you might have only a few hours to paint a particular landscape view.

To paint a subject *alla prima* then, is to respond to your first impression – and in doing so, the painting is likely to be far more spontaneous and authentic than a painting produced from reference in a studio. We know that the authenticity of Cézanne's landscape paintings was due to his direct contact with nature. It is this aspect of painting which has most appeal for those who feel at one with their subject – when confronted by the actual experience of real fields, hills, valleys, rivers and sea. There is also something to be said for the idea of producing a portrait or life study in a single sitting; a rapid and direct response can often be more telling than a painting that has been laboured over numerous sittings. The whole process of painting *alla prima* is of course rather 'hit or miss' and, it can go disastrously wrong, but when things do go well the results are particularly rewarding.

Wet-in-Wet

LEFT *Working boats tend to move from one berth to another without warning. This painting on board was rapidly executed in one sitting of 45 minutes in a failing light.* BELOW *This study of a farm wood-store was painted directly onto a small canvas as a single statement.*
BELOW, RIGHT *This small life study was produced in a single sitting at a two-hour life class.*

Anyone producing an *alla prima* painting must of necessity work wet-in-wet; providing that the pigment can be kept moist, it is not necessary to complete the painting in one session. The drying times of oil paints are such that one applies fresh moist colour into, on top of, and alongside existing wet colour.

It is not a technique which allows for precise linear detail since the merging and blending of colour tends to soften outlines. It is, of course, possible to vary the consistency of the paint, but you need to think in terms of broad blocks of colour rather than sharply delineated forms. It is difficult to correct colour values when working wet-in-wet; it is sometimes necessary to scrape off the colour with a palette knife, before reworking a particular passage of the painting. Alternatively, if the impasto is too thick, you can try blotting off the surface with kitchen paper.

Colour

In the course of teaching art students over the last 30 years, I have on occasion found that certain individuals do possess a kind of intuitive colour sense. Most of us, however, must necessarily learn the hard way – through seeing, understanding and experience. In my view, a complete and thorough understanding of colour accrues gradually over the years, and is not something that can be acquired by reading a few books on colour theory. A proper understanding of colour theory is of course important, but my own appreciation of colour has been achieved primarily by painting directly from nature and by studying the work of master colourists such as Titian, Corot, Turner, Delacroix, Monet, Vuillard, Whistler, Gwen John and others. Moreover, I have become increasingly aware of the fact that colour is always interpretative and, as such, dependent on one's emotional response to the subject at the time of painting.

We know from the experiments of Isaac Newton (1642–1727) that a ray of sunlight passing through a prism produces seven coloured rays: violet, indigo, blue, green, yellow, orange and red. We call this the spectrum, and we see colour in objects that reflect or absorb these rays to a greater or lesser extent. If, for example, white light – which is a mixture of all the colours of the spectrum – is shining directly onto a flat surface which is red, it will reflect mainly red. If, on the other hand, the light falls onto a red ball or apple, which is three-dimensional, it will reflect a variety of other colours as the light is deflected by the curvature of the form. For instance, the area of shadow might be tinged with blue or violet.

Colour only exists in relation to other colours. Bright primary colours, for instance, can change the value of a dull opaque colour, simply by being placed in juxtaposition. We call this phenomenon 'simultaneous contrast'. For this reason, the colours we use in painting must always be considered in relation to one another.

PRIMARY COLOURS

The three primary pigment colours are red, yellow and blue. It is not possible to mix the primaries from other colours on the palette and they are also the base colours for secondary and tertiary colours.

ABOVE *A colour wheel of softly merging primary, secondary and tertiary colours.*

SECONDARY AND TERTIARY COLOURS

Secondary colours are those mixed from the three primaries: orange from red and yellow, green from yellow and blue and violet from red and blue.

Tertiary colours are produced by adding proportionally larger amounts of one primary colour to another.

COMPLEMENTARY COLOURS

The colours which appear opposite each other on the colour wheel are known as 'complementary colours'. The complementary colour of each of the primaries, for instance, is a mixture of the remaining two primaries. Thus green (blue and yellow) is the complementary colour of red, blue the complementary colour of orange (red and yellow) and yellow the complementary colour of violet (red and blue).

Complementary colours are contrasted from light to dark, and from warm to cool. If they are mixed together, however, they cancel each other out – turning to grey or near black.

Hue refers to the compound nature of colour – the redness of red for instance – in degrees of intensity.

RIGHT *A colour exercise exploring complementary colour contrasts.*

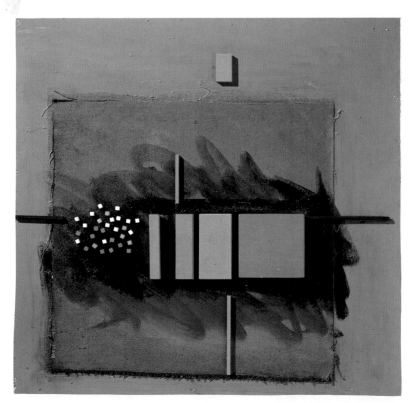

Contrast and Harmony in Colour

There are basically two ways of achieving colour harmony in a painting. Firstly, by using closely related colours, that is to say, colours which are found together on the colour circle. A landscape, for instance, might be painted in a harmony of ochres, siennas and chromes. Secondly, harmony can be attained by carefully contrasting complementaries. Turner, for example, used often to create very subtle harmonies of warm and cool colours in his paintings of landscapes and seascapes.

There is a small painted panel by Walter Sickert that I like very much called 'The Red Shop'. It is a painting of a shop in Dieppe. The shopfront itself is painted in a brilliant shade of Vermilion, but the colour is given much greater intensity by the surrounding drab Ochres, brown and Umber.

A bright colour produces an after-image of its complementary which will affect colours seen in juxtaposition. Colours cannot be considered in isolation, and one is constantly making adjustments to both colour and tonality, as part of the painting process.

A painting that has little or no contrast can often appear flat and dull. The contrast may be very subtle, as in the work of Vuillard, for instance. Conversely, the contrasts can be extremely violent as we see in certain paintings by Van Gogh or in Fauvist paintings such as those by Matisse. Cézanne used contrasts to give his painting greater vibrancy – the repetitive strokes of green which represent the needles of umbrella pines seem to be in continuous movement against the contours of the land mass and sky. When artists talk about the quality of the light they are not

LEFT *Contrasting complementary colours used to heighten the underlying abstract elements of the composition.* OPPOSITE, TOP RIGHT *A successful harmony of colour and tone.* OPPOSITE, FAR RIGHT *A study of Vuillard's, 'The Kitchen, Boulevard Malesherbes', produced to see how the artist used a limited palette of closely-related colours.* OPPOSITE, BOTTOM RIGHT *A harmonious relationship of mid-tones and colours of neutral density creates a pervading calm.*

only referring to the clear bright atmosphere of a sunny day! They are concerned with the way that certain conditions of light enable them to see scales of colour and tone which they must try to capture to produce contrast and harmony in their paintings.

The seeming complexity of contrast and colour will become less bewildering with practice – not just in the handling of materials and techniques, but also when searching for suitable subjects to paint. You have to learn to look properly.

In the small working port of Newhaven, which is a few miles from where I live, I can always be sure that if I walk from the Customs House to the harbour entrance, I will find a series of subjects which are sufficiently stimulating in terms of contrast and colour. The fishing trawlers painted in bright primary colours contrast with the darker tones of the sludge-covered landing stages and the surrounding murky water.

The important thing is to allow oneself to be open to possibilities and to respond before the sensation fades.

Colour Exercises

38 The following exercises might prove useful in helping you to understand the problems of contrast and colour and also ensure that you get into the habit of mixing colours thoroughly with a sense of purpose.

Allow plenty of space for mixing colour. If you do not have a large palette, use a slab of glass on a table. Practise really blending colours together using a palette knife.

❶ *Paint a roughly defined square or rectangle of orange-red on a white ground. Add secondary and tertiary complementary colours as adjacent shapes, working in a purely abstract way so that the first colour is isolated.*

❷ *Mix ten cool greys and ten warm greys arranged as two parallel tonal scales. Make notes of the colours used and keep for future reference.*

A grouping of objects selected at random for their colour value.

3 *See how many objects you can find around the house which are all the same colour but of differing shades and hues. Anything will do – books, items of clothing, fruit and vegetables, ornaments, crockery and so on. Arrange everything in terms of overlapping shapes. Now produce a painting which reduces everything in your arrangement to basic abstract coloured shapes. Make sure that you match colours carefully in terms of intensity and contrast.*

Tone

When you look at great paintings by masters such as Rembrandt, Poussin or Turner, you become aware that everything in their composition is related to an overall tonal scheme. It is usually the case that people who paint badly often have difficulties with tone; it is the tonal qualities which pull the colours in a painting together. For this reason, it is important to understand how tonal values work. If the tone of a colour has been badly judged the colour itself will look wrong – poor colour values can usually be attributed to a lack of tonal unity.

By tone we mean the degree of lightness or darkness of a given colour. Although black and white are not colours – they represent the extremes of the tonal scale.

The French chemist Michel Eugène Chevreul in his experiments to produce modified tones reached 14,440 tones that are measurable. It is important to distinguish between the tone of the actual colour of an object (the local colour), and the tone produced when that same colour is modified by light. Visually, tones are affected by shape, texture and local colour, as well as by distance and by the quality of light.

Colours which are of a different hue might have the same tonal value, so you must give careful consideration to the particular balance of light and dark shapes in painting. In practice, colours will either advance or recede when modified by being made lighter or darker, warmer or cooler.

The artist has produced a harmony of warm and cool greys in this study of Cuckmere Haven in Sussex. Tonal contrasts are clearly defined – the dark headland is seen against a pale sky, and alternating passages of light and dark planes suggest recession on the seashore.

LEFT *A tonal exercise using cut and torn paper overpainted with scumbled colour.*

RIGHT *This painting of an avenue of stones on the ancient site of Olympia in Greece, demonstrates how basic forms are defined by light, colour and tone.*

BELOW *A turbulent sea is represented as a series of interlocking warm and cool tonal planes.*

As an exercise in tonal control, try setting up a still life with a selection of brightly coloured objects against a background paper which is one of the three primaries. Produce a painting of the still life, using only the warm or cool greys that were mixed for the previous colour exercise (see page 39). The main purpose of this exercise is to raise a number of basic questions about the exact relationship between perception and painting. Is it possible, for instance, to register the outline of an object seen against a background of the same tone? How can you represent what you see in reality within the limited range of tones at your disposal? How does light affect tone?

If you do attempt this exercise, you might find that you are more than pleasantly surprised by the results and, more importantly, you will have a much better understanding of tonal values in painting.

Composition

42 The French poet Paul Valéry felt that there were two essential qualities to be found in a work of art: analysis and music. Painters, too, often talk about trying to reconcile the opposing forces of freedom and order in their work. Robert Medley once said that there were two different sides to his pictures: the baroque and the austere: 'I've always found it difficult to reconcile these two extremes. This I suppose is what kept me going.'

Composition – the ordering of elements in a painting – can sometimes start long before any paint has been applied to the canvas. When, for instance, I am searching for a new subject to paint, I am consciously or unconsciously also examining the compositional possibilities. This is particularly true when I am looking for a landscape subject. Landscape is indeterminate and one selects a particular viewpoint because, within the parameters of that view, one is somehow moved or excited by the disposition of elements – trees, rivers, fields, hills and so on.

Having found a suitable subject, you must also take account of the dimensions of the canvas or support in terms of the composition. Matisse once said that his drawings were always related to the given dimensions of the paper and that he would not repeat the same drawing on a sheet of paper of a different size. Some painters – Giacometti for instance – began by painting a loosely defined frame within the canvas area.

All good paintings, no matter how indiscriminate they may seem, are based on an underlying, carefully composed structure. Every element in the painting must count, even though there may be differences of emphasis. The space between objects in a still life, for example, is just as necessary as the objects themselves.

But composition should not be thought of as a convenient means of fitting everything into a preordained plan. Delacroix described composition as the organisation of analogies, taking account of lines, shapes, colour, contrast, tone, rhythm and movement.

As an exercise in composition, a photograph was taken of a field of sheep surrounded by low flint walls. It was framed to show particularly strong shapes.

LEFT *A sketch was made from the photograph suppressing detail and reducing the scene to its basic compositional elements.*

LEFT *A painting was made on site using the sketch as a guide. The emphasis is on the underlying geometry of the composition.*

Scale and Proportion

44

There are a number of simple devices for dividing the picture plane which have been used by painters since the Renaissance. The best known of these divisions is called the Golden Section. The basic premise of the Golden Section is that the proportion of the smaller to the larger is the same as that of the larger is to the whole.

The Fibonacci Series is another method of establishing related proportions, based on the idea that each succeeding number is the sum of the two preceding numbers, i.e. 1.1.2.3.5.8.13.21 and so on. Examples of its use can be found in the work of Piero della Francesca and other Renaissance masters.

LEARNING FROM THE MASTERS

One can gain a much better understanding of composition by making transcriptions from master painters such as Piero della Francesca, Poussin, Vermeer, De Hooch and Seurat. In the study of Vermeer's painting, 'Young Woman In Blue' (1662–64 – 46cm x 39cm/21 x 19 inches), I began by marking the exact dimensions of the original, onto a primed piece of plywood which was 57cm x 60cm/23 x 24 inches, thus allowing a border all round the image. Because I was working from a reproduction which had been scaled down to half size, I had to make the necessary adjustment in my preliminary measurements to get back to the size of the original painting. Working in a soft pencil, I first noted the essential divisions of the picture-plane. When working on a transcription of this kind, you are not concerned with simply making a copy of the painting but rather with trying to uncover through analysis how it was constructed.

The underpainting was done in a bistre of Sepia. As the work progressed I became very conscious of Vermeer's superb sense

LEFT *Transcriptions from Vermeer's 'Young Woman in Blue'. The first study is the same size as the original.* ABOVE *The second study attempts to uncover the relationship between the standing figure and the background.* OPPOSITE *Transcription from Vermeer's 'A Woman Weighing Gold' adapting the proportions to a square canvas.*

THE GOLDEN SECTION

To divide a rectangle using the Golden Section theory, start with a square ABCD. Divide the square in half with line YX. Place a compass point on X and, using B as a radius, describe an arc cutting the extension of line DC at E. Raise an upright from E to meet the extension of the line AB at F. The Golden Section rectangle is AFED. The line BC indicates the Golden Section division.

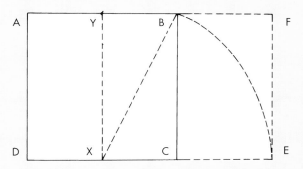

A simple formula can be used to discover the Golden Section point on any line. Take the line AB and raise an upright from it, BD, which is equal to half the distance from A to B. (The point C on AB indicates the halfway point). Draw a line to join A to D.

Now, place a compass point on D and, using B as a radius, describe an arc from B to cut AD at X. Next, place the compass point on A and, using X as a radius, describe another arc to cut AB at GS. This is the Golden Section point.

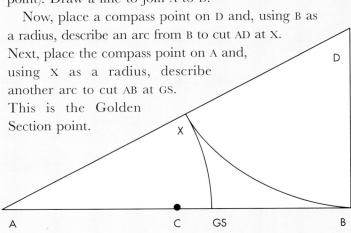

of composition – the exquisite placement and how every element was related to an underlying abstract structure. I became very aware of the negative shapes between objects. The subtle shape created between the back of the figure and the chair on the extreme right, for example. The particular angle of the head is based on a diagonal line which runs from the bottom left-hand corner to a point which marks the Golden Section.

The second study – 'A Woman Weighing Gold' (1662–64, 42cm x 35cm/17 x 14 inches) was painted directly onto a square canvas which was of a different proportion to the original. Here, I was more concerned with extracting the main compositional elements, rather than making a precise transcription. The woman holding a balance in her right hand, maintains the balance of her own posture by touching the table with her left hand.

Rhythm and Movement

ABOVE, LEFT *Tourists hurrying through the Eygptian galleries of the British Museum seem insignificant in relation to the sculpture.*
LEFT *This painting attempts to arrest the movements of the conductor Christof Penderecki.*

Our perception of the world has changed dramatically in the latter part of the twentieth-century. More often than not our experience of landscape is a fleeting glance from the window of a car or train travelling at speed. But more than that, the whole pace of life has changed to such an extent that we tend to scan rapidly rather than pause for any length of time. And yet, all of our sensory experience comes from movement – without movement there is no life. In drawing and painting, we use line to express movement because line transports the eye more rapidly than blocks of colour or flat shapes. The futurist painters, led by the Italian Umberto Boccioni, attempted to render movement in their paintings with unequal success. In their manifesto of 1910, they proclaimed, 'Universal dynamism must be rendered in painting as a dynamic sensation . . . motion and light destroy the materiality of bodies.'

It is difficult to take account of movement while painting from direct observation – and nature is never still, everything is in constant movement, however imperceptible. Horizontal and vertical lines can be used to give an air of stability. Diagonals, because they are off balance, are symbols of motion and suggest continual movement.

I have recently been working on a series of paintings based on the Egyptian Rooms at the British Museum in London. I was interested in the visual dichotomy between the stillness and monumentality of the wonderful artefacts, and the movement of groups of tourists hurrying past. I made some rapid sketches and also took some reference photographs using a fast shutter speed to arrest the movement. From the drawings and colour prints I was able to reconstruct the image on canvas, starting with an underpainting in Sepia.

Some marks were lost and others gained, and it was important to maintain the balance between stillness and movement. It is always easier to start a painting than to know when it is finished. I sometimes leave a painting around for a month or so until I am sure there is nothing to be added or taken away. Sometimes it is a case of making a particular tone lighter or darker. On occasion I have been known to take the most drastic of moves and started a painting again.

LEFT *Because musicians are constantly moving, the artist must react by making rapid judgements visually.* BELOW LEFT *There is an interesting relationship in this painting between the static form of the scuplture and the blurred figure in movement.*

BELOW RIGHT *The vertical structure of walls and pillars provide visual equivalents to the single moving figure.*

Form and Structure

When we talk about structure in painting, we refer both to the underlying organisation of space, using divisions such as the Golden Section, and also to the visible elements of the painting concerned with substance and stability. 'Construction,' said the poet Baudelaire, 'is the framework, so to speak, the surest guarantee of the mysterious life of the works of the mind.'

I have always been interested in the way that man-made artefacts and structures can add dynamism to an otherwise dull scene. On most days, if I walk down to the seafront where I live, I can watch the wooden structures called 'groynes' being bolted together from rough-cut planks of wood. The groynes provide stability, preventing the shingle beach from being shifted away by the tides. The artist is ruled by what he or she sees and while, as a conservationist, one might object to a structure such as an electric pylon being placed in a landscape, as an artist, you might find that such a structure provides the essential link to your composition. I find that industrial landscapes often take on a grandeur that is missing in more conventional landscape subjects. I am interested in both the structural aspect of composition theory and also in subjects which combine man-made structures with natural forms.

LEFT *The wooden structures of the entrance to Newhaven harbour define the space of sea and sky.*

OPPOSITE RIGHT *Industrial artefacts, such as this sand and gravel hopper, can often provide more visual interest than conventional landscape subjects.*

RIGHT *In this painting a steel cable revealed at low tide provides a visual link which the eye follows from the foreground to the boats in the middle-distance.*

BELOW RIGHT *The structural elements in this industrial harbour scene have been carefully selected to produce an interesting composition.*

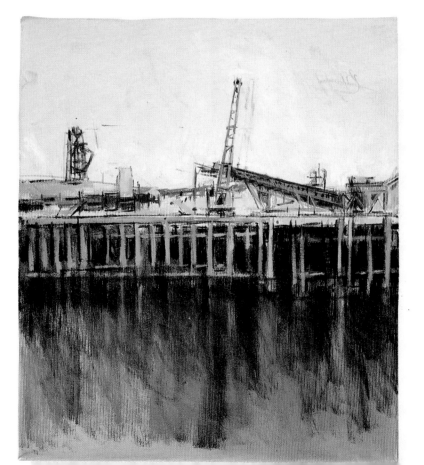

Perspective

Perspective is the means by which we suggest distance and three dimensions in painting. There are a number of different perspective systems, the most important of which for the painter is aerial perspective. Aerial perspective makes use of the gradation of colours to suggest distance. In the wonderfully atmospheric landscapes by Turner, for instance, we see how subdued colour and forms which are less distinct, lead the eye towards cooler and lighter tints, and perhaps the barely perceptible form of a church or castle on a hillside. Leonardo da Vinci in his notebooks referred to the phenomenon of aerial perspective: . . . 'You know that in an atmosphere of uniform density the most distant things seen through it, such as the mountains, in consequence of the greater quantity of atmosphere which is between your eye and them, will appear blue, almost of the same colour as the atmosphere when the sun is in the east.' He goes on to say that buildings in the foreground should be painted their natural colour, and those more distant 'less defined and bluer.'

Linear perspective is often used in conjunction with aerial perspective. The Renaissance architects Brunelleschi and Alberti are generally credited with its invention and it formed the basis of paintings by Piero della Francesca and Signorelli.

Linear perspective is based on the premise that all lines in nature appear to converge as they recede from the spectator and meet at a point on the horizon we call the 'vanishing point'. The eye is on a level with the horizon and, as a consequence, lines which move away from the spectator and are below the eye-level, will move upwards towards the horizon. Lines above the eye-level move in a downward direction to the horizon. In more complex schemes of perspective, there are multiple vanishing points. All perspective systems are a distortion of visual perception, because we do not see everything on a flat surface.

THE PICTURE-PLANE

The picture-plane is an imaginary transparent vertical plane set on the ground and is at that distance from the artist where the painting begins. The artist's exact position behind the picture plane is critical, and when people experience things going wrong it usually has something to do with the eye-level.

If, for instance, you are sitting on the ground, the eye-level will be radically different than if you were standing. Again, if you move to the extreme right or left of the picture-plane there will be a corresponding shift in terms of perspective.

OPPOSITE *In this seascape and landscape, aerial perspective has been employed by adjusting colour and tonal values to suggest recession and distance.*

ABOVE *These two diagrams show how lines which are parallel to each other seem to converge at the vanishing point VP.*

LEFT *The use of linear perspective is evident in these two paintings of Stansted Airport, Essex. The inclusion of a single figure in the compositions provides an added sense of scale.*

Painting from Drawing

There are painters who subscribe to the view that one's work should be carried out in the presence of the subject or motif – what we commonly call 'painting from nature'. There is a lot to commend this point of view; spontaneity and purity of vision are among the qualities we associate with painting directly from the subject. But as Walter Sickert once said, 'do you suppose that nature is going to sit still and wait until you have got what is there?' He reinforces his argument by suggesting that all interesting things that happen in nature are anyway of momentary significance. He cites the fact that Millet made notes on scraps of paper while watching people working in the fields. Very few paintings are literal transcripts from nature and some of the greatest masterpieces were produced by a combination of memory, imagination and varying sources of reference.

The drawings produced as reference for painting are not intended for exhibition. They are, however, of great interest because they show the working of the artist's mind – the first thoughts on the subject. What matters most is that your drawing should have sufficient information for you to be able to develop your painting with conviction. Some artists like to add notes to the drawing to remind themselves of colour values. Thus one finds descriptions such as 'mid-slate', 'buff' or 'brick red', added as footnotes.

Remember that you will have to interpret your drawing in a much broader way with a brush. Most reference drawings are produced 'sight-size' – the scale to which we draw naturally, depending on your distance from the subject. This means that the drawing will have to be enlarged in proportion to the size of the canvas or board.

SQUARING-UP

It is important that the proportion of the drawing and canvas are the same. A drawing on a piece of paper sized 24cm x 28cm/$9^{1/3}$ x $11^{1/5}$ inches, for example, is in direct proportion at 2:5 to a canvas sized 60cm x 70cm/24 x 28 inches. To check the proportion of the drawing against the canvas, draw a diagonal line on the drawing from the bottom left-hand corner to the top right-hand corner. Now draw a similar diagonal on the canvas and place the drawing to fit the bottom left-hand corner of the canvas. Lay a rule or straight-edge along the diagonal – if the top edge of the rule intersects the top right-hand corner of the canvas, it is in proportion.

A grid of squares is overlaid on the original drawing. The same number of squares are measured onto the canvas. It is then possible to match the content of each square of the drawing to the corresponding square on the canvas – so that the original drawing is enlarged. The drawing on the canvas, resulting from this particular method of squaring-up, will almost certainly look very stilted, but it provides a firm basis for making a start on the underpainting.

SICKERT'S METHOD

Instead of scaling up the drawing onto canvas, Sickert preferred to use a thin sheet of paper the same size as the canvas. To transfer the drawing to canvas, he first painted some old newspaper with black oil paint. The painted side of the newspaper was placed in contact with the canvas and the enlarged drawing placed on top. All the lines were then traced through with a hard pencil, which forced a deposit of the black pigment onto the canvas underneath it – rather like a carbon paper.

OPPOSITE FAR LEFT
A landscape drawing that has been squared-up prior to transferring to canvas.

OPPOSITE LEFT *A landscape drawing has been divided by a grid of 16 squares. The corresponding squares are scaled-up in direct proportion to the dimensions of the canvas.*

ABOVE *It sometimes happens that a landscape view seen momentarily on a journey can be drawn quickly and used later as reference for a painting.*

LEFT *This painting was made in the studio from the sketch, the artist having committed colour to memory.*

Painting from Photographs

Despite the fact that artists of the calibre of Degas, Bonnard and Vuillard used photographs for their paintings in the early part of this century, many artists today remain sceptical about such a practice. There are, of course, obvious dangers in that the painting can be nothing more than a slavish copy of purely photographic values. Sickert who also used photographs as reference, once suggested that, rather like alcohol, photography should only be allowed to those who can do without it!

Photographs are most useful as a stabilised source of reference. This is particularly important when we need to record a situation where, for instance, figures are in constant movement, or where one is working against time itself. The English artist Paul Nash (1889–1946), who was forced by illness to rely increasingly on photographic reference, also spoke of the 'peculiar power of the camera to discover beauty'. The viewfinder on a camera is in fact a very useful compositional aid.

This painting of a goatherd was inspired by a visit to a small island near Patmos, Greece. A few rapid sketches and photographs were the only sources of reference. During the course of painting, radical adjustments were made to colour and tone to produce a more brilliant suggestion of the light.

While I sometimes use photographs as reference, I would not use any photographs other than those I have taken myself. For any painting we need to have experience of the event, as well as reference. When painting from a photograph I also have a memory of the event.

The most unsatisfactory aspect of working from photographs I find is that there is not enough information. I see more when working from direct observation than anything registered on photographic film. Additionally, the colour values are levelled out to such an extent that they are misleading. Another difference is that I would rarely add anything to a painting produced from direct observation, but I am constantly making adjustments to paintings produced from photographic reference.

How the Projects Work

58

The first part of this book has dealt with the materials and techniques of oil painting. If we want to realise our subjects and to express our visual experience fully, we must necessarily be able to handle techniques confidently. If, however, we were to be concerned solely with achievement then our work would be completely devoid of imagination.

In the Project Section which follows, you will see how three artists have approached the same subjects in terms of their own personal vision and technique.

The introduction to each of the ten projects attempts to identify the specific problems associated with each project, and suggests possible solutions.

By following the step-by-step progress of each artist you will see how each interprets the project in his or her own way. One artist might succeed in terms of colour, for instance, but be let down by the composition. It is difficult to take account of everything. Sometimes our faults are not immediately apparent until we compare what we have done with the work of someone else who is tackling the same problem. When one of Whistler's pupils said, 'I paint what I see,' Whistler replied, 'Indeed, but just you wait and see what you have painted!'

SOPHIE MASON is a born colourist as is evident in her handling of the series of projects which follow. She is best known for her landscape paintings and enjoys searching for new subjects. Her paintings of Spain demonstrate an acute awareness of the effects of light. She likes to combine media in order to achieve the rich variety of colour and texture which she uses so joyously in her work.

JOHN ARMSTRONG is an experienced painter with considerable knowledge of the craft of painting. He has made a particular study of the working methods of artists of the Italian Renaissance. This he has put to good use in his many commissions for altar pieces for churches in England. He enjoys drawing and painting directly from observation, however, and has recorded the English landscape in all seasons and under varying conditions of light.

Specially devised projects designed to cover popular subjects.

ROBERT WILLIAMS is an artist with a growing reputation for his landscapes of the chalkland areas of southern England. Additionally, his professional work as a conservator of oil paintings has given him a unique insight into working methods and materials.

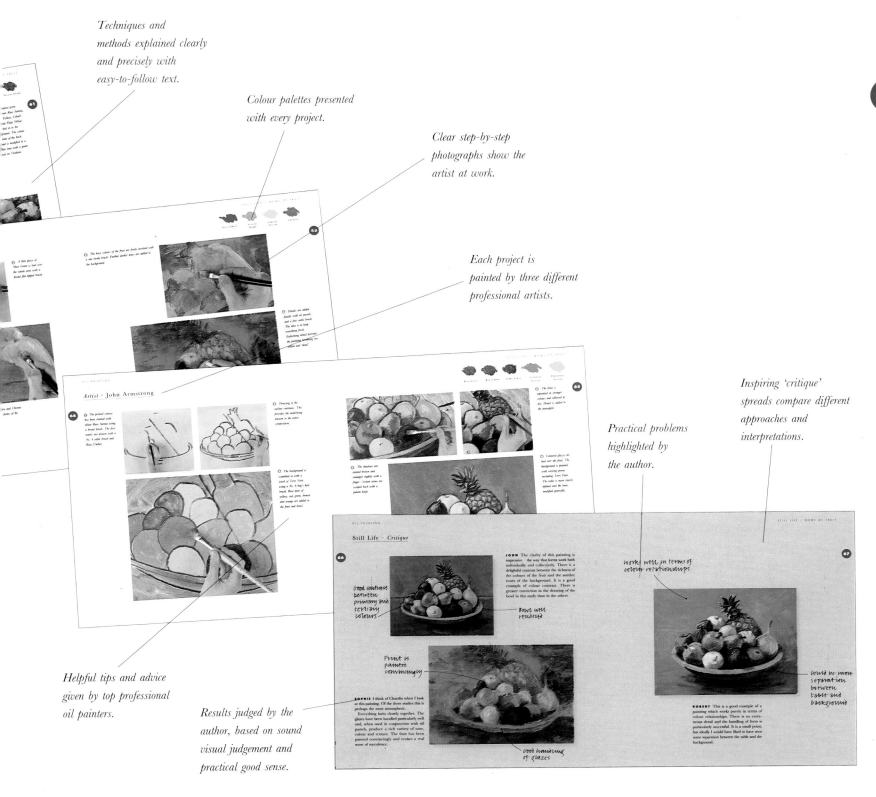

Techniques and methods explained clearly and precisely with easy-to-follow text.

Colour palettes presented with every project.

Clear step-by-step photographs show the artist at work.

Each project is painted by three different professional artists.

Inspiring 'critique' spreads compare different approaches and interpretations.

Practical problems highlighted by the author.

Helpful tips and advice given by top professional oil painters.

Results judged by the author, based on sound visual judgement and practical good sense.

Still Life

BOWL OF FRUIT

A still-life group can be a carefully arranged selection of objects which are of particular interest to the artist, or a random collection of unrelated items thrown together in a haphazard way. Whatever objects you choose, and however they are arranged, try at least to select things that you like. If the still-life group holds no particular interest, then that will inevitably be reflected in the resulting painting.

A bowl of fruit is more than just the sum of parts – each apple or pear has its own individual shape and colour. The success of the painting will depend on just how much you are prepared to invest in trying to uncover the specific values of each inanimate object and the collective values of colour, tone and composition.

The advantage of having everything in a fixed position for a number of days or weeks might be lost if you lose interest after a few hours. It is important, therefore, to determine from the outset what you want to get from the subject. You can pace yourself, for instance, by concentrating on the main structure during the first two sessions, before progressing to colour values during third and fourth sessions. But this will be determined by the complexity of the subject, and the amount of concentrated effort that goes into trying to understand and evaluate the shape and structure of natural forms. Do not have too high an expectation of the finished result, but rather try to gain ground by looking at the subject freshly at the beginning of each session.

Artist • Robert Williams

VANDYKE BROWN

RAW SIENNA

NAPLES YELLOW

COBALT BLUE

VIRIDIAN

YELLOW OCHRE

61

❶ *The ellipses of the bowl and the basic shape of the fruit are carefully drawn with graphite pencil on a primed board. The basic tonal pattern is re-stated on top of the existing drawing with Vandyke Brown using a flat hog's hair brush.*

❷ *A neutral green mixed from Raw Sienna, Naples Yellow, Cobalt Blue and Flake White is blocked in to the background. The colour and tone of the background is modified to a darker tone with a green based on Viridian.*

❸ *Individual fruits are given an undertone of brown and light red. Work continues on the basic colours of the fruit.*

❹ *The rim of the bowl is painted in a pale tone of red where it catches the light. Yellow Ochre and pale green are added to the fruit.*

❺ *All the details and texture are added to the fruit and the contrasting tones of the background and the bowl are further modified.*

Artist • Sophie Mason

1 *The outline shapes of individual fruit and the bowl are loosely sketched in with oil pastels on primed canvas paper.*

2 *A thin glaze of Olive Green is laid over the whole area with a broad flat-tipped brush.*

3 *Darker green glazes are added to provide contrast.*

4 *Warm tints of crimson, Yellow Ochre and Chrome Yellow provide emphasis to the rounded forms of the fruit and bowl.*

OLIVE GREEN   YELLOW OCHRE   CHROME YELLOW   CRIMSON

63

5 *The base colours of the fruit are freely overlaid with a one-stroke brush. Further darker tones are added to the background.*

6 *Details are added finally with oil pastels and a fine sable brush. The idea is to keep everything fresh. Enlivening detail prevents the painting becoming too settled and 'dead'.*

Artist • John Armstrong

64

1 *The primed canvas has been stained with dilute Raw Sienna using a broad brush. The first marks are drawn with a No. 4 sable brush and Raw Umber.*

2 *Drawing of the outline continues. This provides the underlying tension or the entire composition.*

3 *The background is scumbled in with a wash of Terre Verte using a No. 8 hog's hair brush. Base tints of yellow, red, green, brown and orange are added to the fruit and bowl.*

RAW SIENNA   RAW UMBER   TERRE VERTE   CADMIUM ORANGE   PERMANENT YELLOW

65

5 The fruit is repainted in stronger colours and allowed to dry. Detail is added to the pineapple.

4 The shadows are stained brown and smudged slightly with a finger. Certain areas are scraped back with a palette knife.

6 Coloured glazes are laid over the fruit. The background is painted with varying greens including Terre Verte. The table is more clearly defined and the tones modified generally.

Still Life • *Critique*

Good contrast between primary and tertiary colours

Bowl well rendered

JOHN The clarity of this painting is impressive – the way that forms work both individually and collectively. There is a delightful contrast between the richness of the colours of the fruit and the sombre tones of the background. It is a good example of colour contrast. There is greater conviction in the drawing of the bowl in this study than in the others.

Fruit is painted convincingly

Good handling of glazes

SOPHIE I think of Chardin when I look at this painting. Of the three studies this is perhaps the most atmospheric.

Everything knits closely together. The glazes have been handled particularly well and, when used in conjunction with oil pastels, produce a rich variety of tone, colour and texture. The fruit has been painted convincingly and evokes a real sense of succulence.

works well in terms of colour relationships

could be more separation between table and background

ROBERT This is a good example of a painting which works purely in terms of colour relationships. There is no extraneous detail and the handling of form is particularly successful. It is a small point, but ideally I would have liked to have seen some separation between the table and the background.

Glazes and Impasto

VASE OF FLOWERS

How can you interpret the delicacy of flowers in terms of oil painting? There are essentially two approaches to the subject. You can use a combination of thin glazes and fine brushwork or simply try to say something about tonal and colour values using the paint with a broad brush and a rich impasto. If, however, you are concerned with fine detail, then it might be as well to work in another medium, such as watercolour or tempera.

Although there is a long tradition of flower painting, it is not often that one sees really good contemporary examples of the genre. All too often, flower painting is seen as a kind of therapeutic hobby rather than as a subject to be invested with serious visual

analysis. As with all still-life subjects, you have the freedom to select and group objects to suit your purposes and to control the lighting in which they are seen.

It is important to try to retain the vigour and vibrancy of the subject, from the first marks made on canvas to the finished painting. If the painting becomes too laboured at any stage, it should be scraped back and the forms re-stated. The artist must sometimes perform rather like a tightrope walker and a dancer at the same time, to harness exuberant shapes and colour within a disciplined structure. The speed and energy of the brushstroke can contribute to the liveliness of the work.

Artist • Robert Williams

LAMP BLACK   PURPLE LAKE   RAW UMBER   OLIVE GREEN   CADMIUM YELLOW   YELLOW OCHRE

69

❶ *A rough underpainting is made on primed board with a flat hog's hair brush and Lamp Black. A mid-grey defines the undertone of the vase.*

❷ *The background is blocked in with a dark red-brown mixed from Purple Lake and Raw Umber.*

❸ *Various tones of red and Yellow Ochre are used as an under tone on the flowerheads.*

❹ *An Olive Green is applied broadly to delineate leaf shapes. Further colours are added to the flowers.*

❺ *Individual petals and fronds are now finely detailed using the edge of the flat hog's hair brush.*

Artist • Sophie Mason

70

1 *The main outline of the composition is drawn in oil pastel onto primed board. The drawing is tentatively stated to allow for the painting to be developed in terms of colour and tone.*

2 *A rich crimson glaze is brushed over the whole area using a wide one-stroke brush.*

3 *A glaze mixed from Cadmium Orange, Chrome Yellow and Vermilion is laid on a base colour for the flowers. A second glaze of white mixed with Cadmium Yellow is overlaid on the pot and background.*

CRIMSON   CADMIUM ORANGE   CHROME YELLOW   VERMILION   VIOLET   BLACK

4 *The background is made considerably darker with a colour mixed from violet, crimson and black to produce greater contrast. More specific areas of colour are painted fairly thickly using a one-stroke brush.*

5 *Work continues on the flowerheads using contrasting colours and glazes.*

6 *Final details are added to flowers and ferns using a fine sable brush. Oil pastels are also used to produce a variety of tone and contrasting texture.*

Artist • John Armstrong

1 *The primed board is first stained with Indian Red and when dry sand-papered slightly. The general rhythm of the composition is noted with a few strokes of Raw Umber using a No. 4 one-stroke brush.*

2 *The base colour is blocked in using a one-stroke brush. Some colour is wiped off with a tissue.*

3 *The background is painted in a dark magenta using a one-stroke brush. Basic tones are added to the flowerhead and vase. Everything is scraped down slightly.*

INDIAN RED   MAGENTA   RAW UMBER   CHROME YELLOW   OLIVE GREEN

73

4 *The basic geometry of the interlocking shapes is considered. Details are added to petals, grasses and ferns and also to the vase.*

5 *A darker glaze is overlaid on the background with a hog's hair brush. Details are picked out using a fine sable brush.*

6 *The white flowers are painted deftly with Titanium White and a fine sable brush. Finally, the tone and colour of the table is adjusted in relation to the feel of the painting.*

Glazes and Impasto • *Critique*

Background colour could be less opaque

colour tone and detail finely balanced

ROBERT There are similarities between this study and that of John Armstrong. It is handled very competently and with a sound understanding of colour values. It is descriptive without being overly concerned with detail. The tones are well judged and this prevents the painting from being too flat. Again, I feel the background colour could have been less opaque.

JOHN The evocation of delicacy is well handled in this flower study. There is a fine balance between colour, tone and detailed analysis. The warm, dark background colour lends a richness and harmony to the colour scheme generally – though some may feel that it is perhaps a shade too dark.

SOPHIE I like the way that this exuberant study fills the whole canvas. There is an interesting balance between the opaque colour and selected linear detail. Forms are hinted at rather than overstated. Though I feel that this is a particularly successful version of the flower study project, I also like it at its penultimate stage, as a simple colour harmony.

Interesting balance between the opaque colour and selected linear detail

Interior

THROUGH THE WINDOW

The artistic convention of painting a view through a window is almost as old as the history of art itself. It was a favourite device for painters during the Renaissance, and, more recently, for painters such as Bonnard and Matisse. Vermeer and De Hooch also used the open window to create a sense of depth.

Essentially, this kind of painting works on two levels; an interior and exterior spearated by a window or door which acts as a framing device linking inside to outside. It is interesting sometimes to see just how much information can be contained within a tiny division of a window-pane.

The complexity of a view seen through a window should be offset by an interior which is fairly sparse or, conversely, a room that is full of interest should be contrasted with simple forms seen through the window. Of course, adjustments can be made tonally; subdued interior lighting will anyway reduce everything to a simple dark pattern. The position of the artist is fairly critical; the window might take up four-fifths of the picture area, for instance, or be reduced to a diminutive opening on a distant wall.

It is helpful to do a thumbnail sketch to try out the composition before starting the final painting.

Artist • Robert Williams

PRUSSIAN BLUE COOL GREY NEUTRAL GREEN COBALT BLUE CRIMSON

1 *An underpainting is made on primed hardboard using a flat hog's hair brush and blue-black.*

2 *A mid-grey tone serves to establish the basic tonal contrasts. The painting continues to be developed in monochrome.*

3 *A pale neutral green and a darker green define the garden and chair seen though the window.*

4 *A pale glaze of Cobalt Blue is added to the sky, and the flowers in the foreground are suggested by basic blocks of colour.*

5 *All colours and tones are adjusted in relation to each other. The sky is made closer in tone to the distant buildings. Details are added to the garden and the flowers are brought into sharper focus in terms of contrast and detail.*

Artist • Sophie Mason

78

❶ *The main structure of the window and the position of the plant are drawn on primed board using crimson and brown oil pastels.*

❷ *A thin glaze of crimson is overlaid on areas seen though the window and on the plant using a broad brush. This establishes the basic abstract pattern of the painting.*

❸ *A glaze of ultramarine is laid over the sky area, and as a pale shadow on parts of the window.*

❹ *Further glazes of pale blue-purple are added to the sky and distant buildings seen through the window. A pale blue mixed from Cobalt Blue, Titanium White and a touch of crimson, is painted onto the window frame. At this stage, tones are fairly even.*

BURNT UMBER   CRIMSON   ULTRAMARINE   COBALT BLUE   VIRIDIAN   TURQUOISE

5 *A glaze of Burnt Umber provides contrast and isolates the plant.*

6 *The plant is loosely re-stated using further glazes, and oil pastels. A further glaze of turquoise is laid over the garden area. The artist has decided that, in order to retain the fluidity of colour and the vividness of the light, the painting should be considered finished at this point.*

Artist • John Armstrong

80

1 *The canvas is first stained with dilute Cobalt Blue and allowed to dry. The basic outlines are drawn with a No. 4 sable brush and Indigo.*

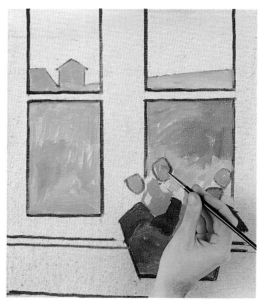

2 *Background tones are defined in flat blocks of grey and green and the flowers given an undertone of pink.*

3 *The flat tones of the window frame and sky are blocked in with a one-stroke brush.*

COBALT BLUE INDIGO LIGHT PURPLE MID-GREY CARMINE PINK

4 *The detail of the window frame is rendered tonally, and the petals of the flowers are more carefully defined.*

5 *Details seen through the window frame, such as the garden chair, are painted with a No. 4 sable brush. Tones are adjusted generally and more detail added to flowers and leaves.*

6 *Using a No. 4 sable brush, the forms are more finely delineated. Additionally, the sense of distance is made more convincing by establishing separate planes of colour.*

Interior • *Critique*

competently handled but rather uninspired

SOPHIE It has not been the artist's intention in this painting to deal with the three-dimensional aspect of the subject. Scumbled colour and thin glazes with dabs of opaque pigment all combine to create the sensation of light values which are constantly shifting from one moment to the next.

ROBERT This is a fairly 'matter-of-fact' interpretation of the subject which has been competently handled. Everything has been sorted out in terms of colour and tone. One has the feeling that it is not a subject for which the artist has much empathy.

Effective use of glazes and scumbled colour

A convincing study

Details seen through the window are rendered convincingly

Flowers painted with conviction

JOHN The flowers in this study have been translated with conviction and the view through the window is better considered than in other paintings. But one feels that the subject itself has not caused much excitement and, as a consequence, this is a rather factual transcription of the scene.

Sky Study

CLOUDS

In many landscape paintings the sky is often treated as a featurless flat block of colour and yet, more than any other element, it can greatly influence the whole mood or drama of a painting. The sky has a structure which is elusive and constantly changing – ponderous clusters of cumulus clouds might break, accumulate and disperse altogether within a short space of time.

The English painter John Constable (1776–1837) once said that, 'the landscape painter who does not make his skies a very material part of his composition neglects to avail himself of one of his greatest aids.' Indeed, he felt that the sky was the keynote in his painting which often determined the mood or sentiment of his composition.

It is precisely because clouds are unfamiliar shapes which are constantly changing that we need to observe them with a greater degree of concentration. Clouds have their own vaporous forms which can be seen to recede in perspective; it is not difficult to observe how their size seemingly reduces in scale towards the distance. Most painters find it useful to make rapid notations using a pencil and sketchbook. The sketches can be kept for reference. In drawing clouds, you need to take account of the duality of translucence and semi-opacity which in turn has to be translated in terms of glazes and impasto. Some painters prefer to work on a coloured ground so that it is easier to deal with the properties of colour, tone and structure of cloud compositions.

Artist • Robert Williams

COBALT BLUE

ULTRAMARINE

ALIZARIN CRIMSON

PRUSSIAN BLUE

LAMP BLACK

GREY

85

1 *The complexity of the cloud formation, seen in perspective, is first resolved in terms of a pencil drawing on primed hardboard.*

3 *A strong contrasting tone for the sea is brushed in with a flat hog's hair brush and a mixture of Prussian Blue and Lamp Black.*

2 *The clouds are defined by a pale tone of blue mixed from Cobalt Blue, Titanium White and a hint of Ultramarine.*

4 *The undersides of the clouds are feathered and scumbled with a pale purple mixed from Alizarin Crimson, Ultramarine and Titanium White.*

5 *The painting is now resolved in terms of aerial perspective – with the headland in the distance barely discernible as a pale warm grey. The clouds are not fully resolved in terms of contrast, colour and texture. The tone of the sea is modified in relation to other colours.*

Artist • Sophie Mason

2 *A glaze mixed from Ultramarine and turquoise is laid over the whole area with a broad brush. It is important to get some colour onto the canvas quickly. As soon as the first colours are laid, a whole new set of propositions occur.*

1 *The outline shapes of clouds, headland and sea are drawn in oil pastel onto a primed board.*

3 *Passages of Ultramarine are applied thinly to the sky and sea using a one-stroke brush.*

ULTRAMARINE

TURQUOISE

WARM GREY

PINK

87

5 *A pink-grey tone is painted selectively on the clouds and lighter passages are re-stated.*

4 *Further thin glazes of contrasting blues are added to the sky. The headland and the underside of the clouds are painted in a neutral warm grey.*

6 *Finally, oil pastels are used to create the fluffy texture of the clouds and to express their movement.*

Artist • John Armstrong

❶ *The primed board has been stained with dilute blue with just a tinge of red and allowed to dry. The main outlines are drawn in Cobalt Blue, using a No. 4 sable brush.*

❷ *The dark tone of the sea is mixed from Cobalt Blue, Payne's Grey and Burnt Sienna and blocked in with a No. 8 hog's hair brush. Further tones of mid-grey are added to the headland and the underside of the clouds using a No. 4 sable brush.*

❸ *Dark and light tones of Cobalt Blue are added to the sky. Part of the colour is scraped away before beginning the next stage.*

COBALT BLUE

PAYNE'S GREY

BURNT SIENNA

LIGHT GREY

WARM GREY

4 *The underside of the clouds is scumbled with light and dark grey. The colour is rubbed with a finger afterwards.*

5 *Clouds are repainted using a sable brush and a soft rag. The tone is made paler on the horizon.*

6 *A warm grey has been glazed over the sea and the white of the clouds painted thickly with a No. 4 sable brush. Even in the final stage, the brushwork is kept free to retain the spontaneity of the first stages.*

Sky Study • *Critique*

Experienced handling of cloud types

ROBERT Looking at this painting one feels that the artist is someone who studies cloud types. Again, it works well in terms of light and aerial perspective. The formation of clouds is, I feel, better resolved in the foreground than in the distance.

works well in term light and aerial perspective

JOHN This is a good example of the way that aerial perspective can be used to suggest depth and recession in painting. By carefully modulating the colour and tone of the clouds, sea and distant headland, the artist has presented a convincing interpretation of the subject. The seemingly intangible nature of this kind of nebulous strata is difficult to cope with in any medium, but here the artist has concentrated all his effort on getting it right, judging light against dark and colour against tone.

Good example of aerial perspective

Paint and
pastels combined

Symbolic
rather than
realistic

SOPHIE The artist has dealt with the
subject in her own terms, using a combination of oil paints and oil pastels, to
produce a cloud study which captures
something of the process of transmutation.
One feels that she has been more
concerned with symbolism than with
directly perceived realism.

Nature Study

TREES

Sir George Beaumont once asked Constable, 'do you not find it very difficult to determine where to place your brown tree?' 'Not in the least,' replied Constable, 'for I never put such a thing into a picture.' We sometimes crudely and unthinkingly tend to categorise our visual experiences in terms of convenient clichés. Tree forms are as unique and individual as human forms, and to draw or paint them requires the same degree of concentration that you would expect to find in a life class.

Constable also said that we see nothing until we truly understand it. All too often one's preconceptions of what a tree ought to look like get in the way of real discovery. It is important to remember that each tree is firmly rooted in the ground as a grow-ing organic form. The verticality of its structure is complementary to predominantly horizontal landscape forms. A tree seen in winter, when it has shed its leaves, will look different in high summer, when the abundant foliage will create an entirely different outward shape.

When looking at a drawing or painting of trees you can sometimes see exactly where the artist's interest has tailed-off; lapses in concentration result in clumsy execution in the drawing of branches and leaves. Any tree study, however, must be a summary of things seen – excessive detail often conceals far more than it reveals. Try to capture the main thrust of the trunk and main branches without worrying too much about individual leaves.

Artist · Robert Williams

WARM GREY

COOL GREY

INDIGO

LAMP BLACK

RAW SIENNA

OCHRE

❶ *Two thin glazes of warm and cool grey make the pale background tone. The low horizon line is established and the basic shape of distant trees suggested by a roughly blocked-in grey mixed from Indigo, Lamp Black, Titanium White and a touch of Raw Sienna.*

❷ *The basic structure of the tree is painted with a hog's hair brush in midgrey. A darker grey is added to the foreground.*

❸ *The rough basic shape of the foliage is overlaid in pale Ochre and the sun is registered on the horizon.*

❺ *Tones are further modified to produce a 'contre jour' effect (against the light). Details are added to the copse of trees in the distance.*

❹ *The tone on the horizon is made warmer and further details added to the tree.*

Artist • Sophie Mason

94

❶ *An outline drawing of the tree is made directly onto primed canvas using oil pastel.*

❷ *A thin transparent glaze of crimson is brushed over the surface with a broad one-stroke brush.*

❸ *Glazes of Burnt Umber and violet are painted in the foreground and as a lighter tone in the background.*

CRIMSON   BURNT UMBER   VERMILION   VIOLET   GREY

95

4 *Burnt Umber is added to the tree and as a pale uneven tone over parts of the sky.*

5 *The sun is painted white on the horizon, further glazed passages are added selectively in crimson, Vermilion and Burnt Umber.*

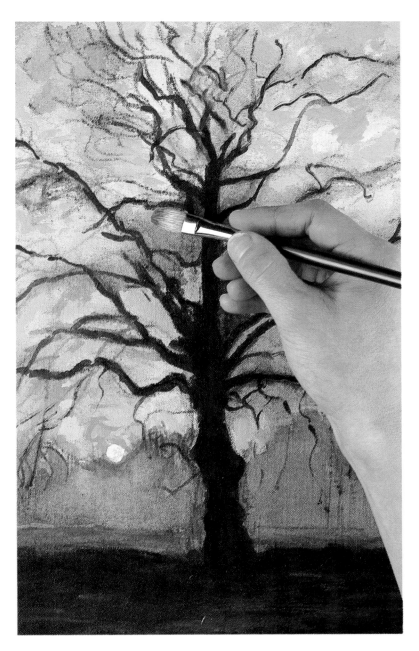

6 *Contours are softened and more detail added to branches of the tree. Details are also added sparingly to the trees in the background.*

Artist • John Armstrong

96

❶ *A coloured ground is produced with a stain of Payne's Grey and allowed to dry. The tree is drawn in a deep blue using a No. 4 sable brush.*

❷ *A mid-grey is blocked into the disant trees using a one-stroke brush. A dark tone is added to the foreground.*

❸ *The tone of the sky is produced by mixing Cobalt Blue, red and white. A warmer tone of orange-pink is painted on the horizon. The grey of the distant trees is smudged with a rag.*

PAYNE'S GREY   INDIGO   COBALT BLUE   CADMIUM RED   CADMIUM YELLOW

4 *Work continues on the branches of the tree.*

5 *Dry brushwork using a hog's hair brush adds depth.*

6 *All the tones are now finally modulated and more dry brush-strokes are added to the extremities of the branches. A lighter tone is painted between branches using a one-stroke brush.*

Nature Study • *Critique*

JOHN The blend of warm and cool hues in this painting produces a strongly atmospheric evocation of a wintry scene. Dry brushwork has been employed successfully to suggest the movement of branches. The tonal recession works well and I feel that this is a straightforward and unpretentious rendering of the subject.

well composed

The tonal recession works well

SOPHIE The tree-form is well composed within the dimensions of the canvas. The subject is treated in a semi-abstract way, reminiscent of Mondrian's tree studies. The branches of the tree serve to define loosely stated areas of colour. It is a painting which goes beyond being a factual recording of the subject, impinging more on the artist's emotional responses to the theme.

Good use of closely-related tones

ROBERT Robert has responded to the subject by producing a harmonious – almost monochromatic – rendering of closely related tones. The pallid wintry light adds just a touch of warmth to the cooler colours used in the rest of the painting. Silhouetted forms, such as the tree, are difficult to handle, and every branch needs to be expressed with conviction to prevent the whole thing drifting into formlessness.

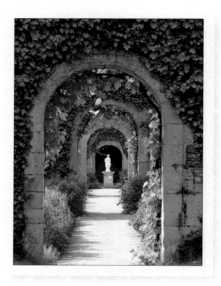

Perspective

FORMAL GARDEN

The formal aspect of a landscaped garden presents the artist with an interesting subject in terms of composition. Harmony of line, proportion and balance are inherent in the best of such gardens, many of which have been modelled on the work of Sansovino and Palladio in Italy, and on Le Nôtre's creations for Louis XIV's Versailles in France. These gardens were laid out in accordance with the rules of classical symmetry. Loggias, statuary, topiary, fountains and dividing walls provide visual incidents which offset the severity of the geometric plan.

When painting a garden scene, consideration should be given to colour and contrast to heighten the formal qualities rather than conceal them. Perspective, of course, plays a vital part in representing the spatial dimension of formal gardens. The choice of viewpoint and selected eye-level can also significantly effect the success or failure of the painting.

Artist • Robert Williams

 LAMP BLACK
 VIRIDIAN
 GERANIUM LAKE
 FRENCH ULTRAMARINE
 NAPLES YELLOW
 YELLOW OCHRE

❶ *The main structure of the arches seen in perspective is rendered as an underpainting using a No. 6 long flat hog's head bristle and Lamp Black on primed hardboard, firmly establishing the composition.*

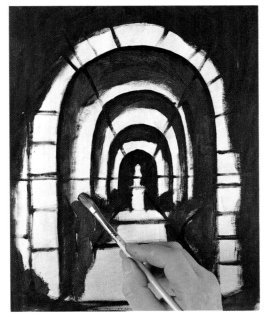

❷ *Working from dark to light the darkest tones, mixed from Lamp Black and Viridian, are applied as a thin but dense layer with a hog's hair bristle brush.*

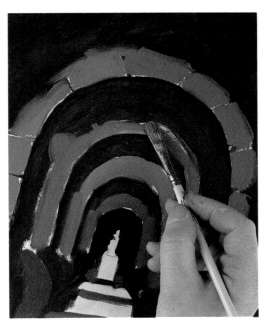

❸ *The stonework of the arches is painted with mid-toned mauve mixed from Geranium Lake and French Ultramarine.*

❹ *The basic shapes of the overhanging vines, shrubs and foliage are roughly established with a pale green mixed from Viridian, Flake White and a touch of Naples Yellow. The path leading to the statue is blocked in with a neutral tint of ochre modified by Titanium White.*

❺ *Everything is given much greater definition, including detail on the stonework, flowers, shrubs and the statue. Contrasts of light and shadow are more sharply represented.*

Artist • Sophie Mason

102

① *The arches are freely drawn in oil pastel onto a primed board.*

② *A glaze mixed from grey and French Ultramarine is laid over the whole area using a broad flat-tipped brush.*

③ *A thin glaze mixed from French Ultramarine and Hooker's Green separates the arches and provides a base colour for the foliage.*

WARM GREY

FRENCH
ULTRAMARINE

HOOKER'S GREEN

TURQUOISE

GERANIUM LAKE

4 *Tones are darkened around the arches and the path picked out in a tint of opaque turquoise.*

5 *The broad underlying shapes of the foliage are established with a one-stroke brush and the recesses are darkened generally.*

6 *The whole painting is given greater contrast and a sense of depth. More brilliant colour is added to the foliage and to garden flowers, using a fine sable brush. Other forms are heightened with tentative strokes of oil pastel crayons.*

Artist • John Armstrong

1 *The primed board is first stained with a dilute mix of Payne's Grey and Cobalt Blue. The first tentative marks are made in Raw Umber using a No. 4 sable brush.*

2 *The sequence of four arches and the distant statue are drawn in perspective with dilute Raw Umber.*

3 *Titanium White, Raw Umber and Cobalt Blue are mixed to produce a blue-grey for the stone arches. A base tone for the foliage is mixed from Terre Verte, Cobalt Blue, Raw Umber and a touch of white.*

PAYNE'S GREY   COBALT BLUE   RAW UMBER   TERRE VERTE   WARM GREY   SPECTRUM RED

4 *Details are added to the greenery with a No. 4 sable brush. Contrasting tones of grey are painted over the path.*

5 *The statue is painted a grey-white.*

6 *Final details are added to flowers with touches of Spectrum Red and highlights added to foliage with a fine sable brush.*

Perspective • *Critique*

Lack of contrast makes the painting appear rather flat

JOHN The painting is handled competently in terms of perspective and composition – I would like to have seen more contrast between the arches as they recede into the distance. Nevertheless, there is a feeling of light and space, and flowers and foliage are painted with understanding.

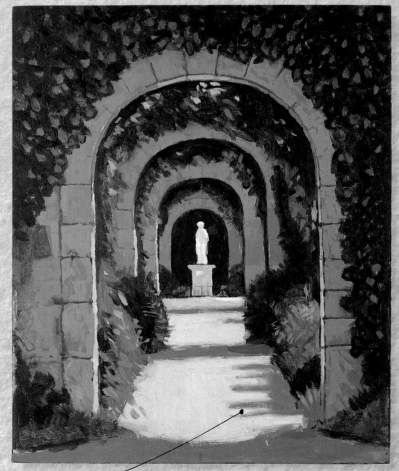

SOPHIE The light in this painting is more subdued – perhaps too much so. The coloration works well in terms of balanced hues of blue and green. Although the painting has a certain presence, the lack of contrast precludes any sense of depth of recession.

Good feeling for light and space

sense of
recession is
convincing
in this
study

ROBERT There is a palpable sense of recession through the arches to the distant statue. The contrasts of light and shade, tone and colour, have been carefully judged so that the eye is drawn towards the centre of the composition.

Landscape

SUNSET IN THE MOUNTAINS

The Cumbrian mountains seen at sunset provide the inspiration for the landscape project. Towards dusk, the failing light negates distance and seemingly reduces everything to a flat, two-dimensional pattern.

Hill farmers in this part of England build drystone walls which follow the contours of hills and valleys. Working with an assortment of stones in different shapes and sizes, they skilfully fit the stones together in such a way that the wall is of even height and width. I mention this because the artist is faced with a task that is analagous to that of the hill farmer. Basic shapes which are symbols for the sun, sky, mountains and forest must be fitted together to form an interlocking harmonious composition.

The word symbol comes from the Greek *sumbolon* which means token. We are able to recognise and accept certain basic shapes as being representative of our wider visual experience. So that to depict forms symbolically, we must show their most characteristic silhouette. If the shapes are difficult to identify, we risk failure in communicating exactly what we wanted to say about the subject. In a project of this kind it is important to produce a satisfactory underlying design before starting to paint.

Artist • Robert Williams

PRUSSIAN BLUE

BLACK

LIGHT PURPLE

COOL GREY

CADMIUM ORANGE

1 *The truncated contours of the mountains are represented as flat shapes of colour. A flat hog's hair brush is used to block in rich warm blues and a blue-black.*

2 *A pinkish-grey and light purple are added to the sky, isolating the sun on the horizon.*

3 *The sun and the light radiating from it are evoked in terms of gradated colour. All the colour and tone of the landscape and sky is modified through the subtle blending of colours of the same hue.*

4 *Trees in the foreground are rendered as silhouettes without being too conspicuous.*

109

Artist • Sophie Mason

2 *A crimson glaze is stained over the whole area using a broad flat-tipped brush.*

1 *The outline forms of the mountains are loosely sketched in oil pastel onto primed board.*

3 *Thin glazes of French Ultramarine, Cobalt Blue and Alizarin Crimson are overlaid on the mountains and foreground. In order to control the development of the painting, the artist allows the tonal values to accrue gradually.*

ALIZARIN
CRIMSON

COBALT BLUE

FRENCH
ULTRAMARINE

COOL GREY

RAW UMBER

5 *A thin, dark glaze is added to the sky to create drama and contrast. The colours of the mountains are intensified.*

4 *Tones are modulated in relation to each other, with the darkest tone in the foreground.*

6 *Details are added with oil pastels. Further glazes are also added to mountains and to the forest in the foreground.*

Artist · John Armstrong

1 *The primed board has been stained with dilute scarlet and allowed to dry. The contours of the mountain are briefly stated in blue using a No. 4 sable brush.*

2 *The mountains are blocked in with a colour mixed from Payne's Grey, Violet and Titanium White. The sun is painted as a white disc on the horizon.*

3 *A grey-blue is added to the sky and when dry, a second glaze mixed from Vermilion and Chrome Yellow and white is laid on top.*

SCARLET PAYNE'S GREY VERMILION VIOLET CHROME YELLOW CADMIUM ORANGE COBALT BLUE

113

4 *A Scarlet glaze is laid over the painting with a hog's hair brush.*

5 *The glaze over the sky is repainted, wiping out the area near the sun. A Cadmium Orange glaze is painted around the sun.*

6 *An impasto of a darker tone is added to the mountains using a palette knife.*

Landscape • *Critique*

subtle blending of colour and tone

ROBERT In a landscape such as this, the distances involved are discerned through veils of pellucid atmosphere which moderates colour and tone. In this painting the artist has dealt with this aspect more convincingly than the others. It requires the ability to blend colour and tone in a very subtle way.

SOPHIE In her interpretation, the artist has sought to provide some sense of animation to an otherwise dull scene. By adding texture to mountains and sky with strokes of oil pastel, she has gone some way to improve the quality of the painting. But the problem remains more fundamental in terms of the chosen viewpoint and composition. Perhaps a different vantage point would have produced a more dramatic picture.

could have chosen a better viewpoint

Is there enough interest?

Good colour harmony

JOHN Here the truncated shapes of the mountains are reduced almost to abstraction. The colour is a harmony of warm colours and tones, with the setting sun remaining the only point of focus – is there enough happening in this painting? Would it be improved, for instance, by adding a single vertical element?

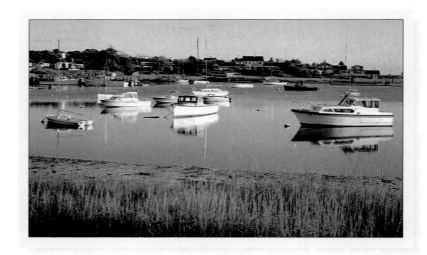

Travel

BOATS AT ANCHOR

A flotilla of pleasure craft at anchor in the still waters of a New England inlet provides a suitable vehicle for testing an artist's ability to bring all the diverse elements together into a meaningful composition. Still water produces mirror-images which add another dimension to the painting by accentuation.

The shapes of boats are deceptive and sometimes difficult to draw. Seen from varying angles, the structure is further complicated by the curve around the hull and from prow to stern. Additionally, there are cabins, rigging and masts to take into account.

When drawing or painting this kind of subject, selection is all important; the harbour may be full of boats, but the particular disposition of these elements in your composition is what counts. You do not have to register everything; if it helps your composition to leave out one or more boats altogether, then there is no particular virtue in keeping them in simply because they are there. It is worth remembering that the artistic values of a painting are independent of the subject – one does not need to be interested in sailing, or even to like boats, to find them useful in constructing a satisfying and enjoyable picture.

You must learn to translate what you experience when confronted by nature – to convey something of the immediacy of the subject and of the shifting values of light and shade.

Artist • Robert Williams

CADMIUM GREEN   LAMP BLACK   YELLOW OCHRE   FRENCH ULTRAMARINE   INDIAN RED   COOL GREY

1 *The composition and basic tonal pattern is resolved in an underdrawing made with a soft graphite pencil on primed board.*

2 *The tree line on the horizon is blocked in with a green-black mixed from Lamp Black and Yellow Ochre. A warm blue based on French Ultramarine isolates the boat shapes.*

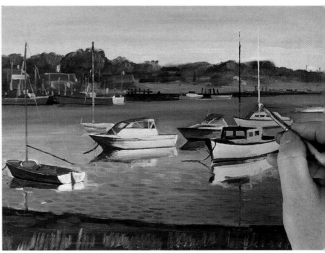

3 *Further blues are applied as thin glazes and Indian Red added to the shoreline. Work continues on the shoreline, foreground and shadows on the boats.*

4 *Mid-tones of warm and cool greys, white and Yellow Ochre provide tonal contrast.*

5 *Details on the boats, such as masts and cabins, are highlighted using the edge of a flat hog's hair brush. Reflections and the effect of dappled water are expressed by stippling, and tones are finally modified in relation to each other.*

Artist • Sophie Mason

118

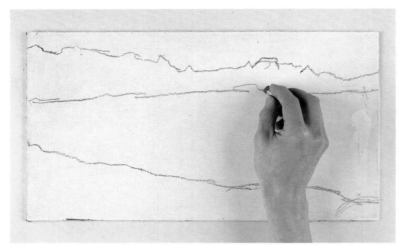

① *The mainland and harbour are defined with oil pastels on primed board.*

② *Glazes of lilac and grey are overlaid with a broad one-stroke brush.*

③ *The mainland is glazed with a colour mixed from Yellow Ochre and Olive Green.*

YELLOW OCHRE OLIVE GREEN LILAC WARM GREY ULTRAMARINE VIOLET BLACK

119

5 *The tone of the sky is darkened considerably using a colour mixed from black, violet and Ultramarine. Olive Green and Yellow Ochre are added to the mainland. The boat shapes are established using a mixture of Ochre and white and darker tones are overlaid on the water.*

4 *The shapes of the boats are drawn over the dried blue glaze using yellow oil pastel.*

6 *Final details are added using oil pastels on grasses in the foreground and for added texture to the sky.*

Artist • John Armstrong

1 *A thin wash of Payne's Grey is applied to the primed board and allowed to dry. The main outlines are drawn in a colour mixed from Terre Verte and Burnt Umber using a No. 4 sable brush.*

2 *The middle-distance is blocked in with a deep olive using a one-stroke brush. The basic shapes of the boats are painted in mid-grey. The fore-ground is added using a green mixed from Yellow Ochre and deep olive.*

3 *The sky and water are painted in mid-blue which is scraped back. If the artist feels a painting has become unworkable, it is necessary to scrape off pigment and re-state the drawing.*

PAYNE'S GREY COBALT BLUE TERRE VERTE BURNT UMBER YELLOW OCHRE OLIVE GREEN MID-GREY

121

4 *Further tones of Ochre and grey are added to the distant harbour. Details such as masts on the boats are painted in white using a fine, short-handled sable brush.*

5 *The sky is made lighter on the horizon. Reflections of the boats are painted with a one-stroke brush and then smudged slightly.*

6 *The foreground is glazed in brown and reeds are added with a fine brush using a dry brush technique. Final details are added to the boats and to their images reflected in the water.*

Travel • *Critique*

SOPHIE The colour and pervading mood of this painting is quite different from the others. The sky, for instance, appears menacing rather than radiant. The light is concentrated on the boats so that they appear to be spotlit in an almost theatrical way.

The artist has taken the subject beyond mere description and has managed to imbue the whole composition with a kind of sombre tranquillity.

Good sombre mood

Boats well lit

Everything is too symmetrical

Good feel for light

JOHN The radiance of light in this painting has been handled well in terms of the medium. Compositionally, the disposition of various elements might seem too evenly balanced, though one might feel that the subject demands this kind of equilibrium. The treatment of boats and their reflections is convincing and the interaction between warm and cool tones of land and sea is interesting.

convincing
handling
of water
and reflection

Good
composition

ROBERT One is immediately struck by the handling of water and reflections in this study – in this sense it is more convincing than the others. The artist has also given more consideration to the composition eliminating some things to produce a better spatial relationship between elements.

A Change of Scene

PROVENÇAL CHAPEL

The Alpilles form a limestone ridge between Avignon and Arles in France – this is Van Gogh country. The outcrops of white rock sharply contrast with the sky, olive groves and cypress trees. The twelth-century chapel of St-Sixte is situated a few kilometres from the small town of Eygalières. It is built on high ground on the site where once stood a pagan temple dedicated to the spirit of the local spring water.

It is always difficult, I feel, to paint in a location which is closely identified with the work of a well-known artist. One tends to view the subject through the eyes of that artist. This project is concerned with very basic compositional problems – the chapel and surrounding walls and trees are fairly simple forms seen in an elevated position. Therefore, the viewpoint can be critical. One needs to walk around the chapel to view it from different angles before deciding on the viewpoint which best brings out the right balance of horizontal and vertical forms.

It is also a subject which, seen under direct sunlight, produces stark contrasts. Therefore, choosing the right time of day can also enhance the subject, greatly influencing the colour and tonality of the painting. The subject seen at midday, for example, would correspondingly require colours to be mixed in a fairly high key – light excludes colour. Brilliant sunlight tends to not only emphasise contrasts but also reduces the contrast between local colours. Generally, you should avoid contradictory effects of light and colour.

Artist • Robert Williams

PRUSSIAN BLUE   LAMP BLACK   FRENCH ULTRAMARINE   ALIZARIN CRIMSON   RAW UMBER   YELLOW OCHRE   CHROME YELLOW

125

❶ *All the compositional details are first resolved by producing an underdrawing on primed board with a graphite pencil. The darkest tones – the cypress trees, and shadows – are painted with a mixture of Prussian Blue / Lamp Black using a hog's hair brush.*

❷ *A pale warm tone of blue mixed from French Ultramarine, Titanium White and a hint of Alizarin Crimson is blocked in to the sky.*

❸ *A band of strongly contrasting tone of green-brown, mixed from Raw Umber with a touch of Lamp Black and Yellow Ochre, is painted in the foreground.*

❹ *An Olive Green mixed from Chrome Yellow and Lamp Black is added to the foreground area in front of the church. The painting is now resolved in an almost monochromatic way, blending colours of the same hue. Textural details are accentuated in the grass, trees and stonework, producing a harmonious tonal quality.*

Artist • Sophie Mason

1 *The trees, landscape and church are drawn with Viridian and Yellow Ochre oil pastels onto ready-primed canvas board. The space around and between objects is also considered.*

2 *Thin glazes of blue and Olive Green are overlaid on the sky and foreground using a one-stroke brush. Here the artist is trying to establish middle tones.*

3 *Darker glazes of green are added to trees and foreground.*

VIRIDIAN

YELLOW
OCHRE

OLIVE GREEN

COBALT BLUE

FRENCH
ULTRAMARINE

RAW UMBER

4 *The tone of the sky is made darker with Cobalt Blue and French Ultramarine and a warm grey added to the church and adjacent walls. A dark Umber is painted in the recess of the doorway.*

6 *The outcrop of limestone in the middle-distance is radically altered to a much lighter tone. Final details are added to the sky, church and trees.*

5 *The tones in the middle-distance and foreground are darkened with shades of Olive Green.*

Artist • John Armstrong

1 *The primed board is stained with Payne's Grey and Cobalt Blue and allowed to dry.*

2 *The main composition is drawn in Raw Umber using a No. 4 sable brush.*

3 *A deep olive colour is overlaid on the foreground and trees, using a hog's hair brush.*

PAYNE'S GREY　　COBALT BLUE　　RAW UMBER　　OLIVE GREEN　　YELLOW OCHRE　　TERRE VERTE　　BURNT SIENNA

4 *The sky is roughly blocked in with blue and when dry scraped down with a flat blade.*

5 *The white wall adjacent to the chapel is painted, details are added to trees and the grass area in the foreground made lighter in tone.*

6 *The sky is painted again and the tone of the ground in the middle-distance made much lighter. Final details are added to the chapel and a palette knife is used to apply more colour in the foreground.*

A Change of Scene • *Critique*

ROBERT The tree on the left-hand side of the middle-distance provides a balance to the whole composition, which has been well considered. The coloration of the painting is a kind of harmony of middle tones, which is particularly suited to the subject. The freshness of handling has been maintained throughout.

colour harmony is suited to subject

Good underlying design

JOHN The light has been concentrated on the chapel and the outcrop of lime-stone, so that all attention is focused directly on the main elements of the composition. It is the underlying abstract values in this painting which make it work as a series of interlocking shapes. Every-thing it seems has been pared down to bare essentials. The artist has managed to resist the temptation of veering towards the picturesque.

SOPHIE There is nothing static about this painting and one feels that the artist has come very close to the spirit of the place. It has a strong rhythmic quality which recalls Van Gogh's paintings of cornfields (which were painted in the same locality). In my view, however, there is an underlying structural weakness in the composition; elements within it appear to be much too compressed. I feel that the main interest for the artist has been in the painting of the sky.

Portrait

MAN IN A TURBAN

In his journal of 1850, Delacroix noted that, 'the warmer the light tones are the more nature exaggerates the contrast with grey: witness the half-tints in the Arabs and in people of coppery complexion.' One feels he could almost have been describing the subject chosen for this portrait.

We tend to see things in terms of contrast – the brilliant lemon yellow of the turban against the background and the leathery tone of the face. We normally think of portrait painting as an interior subject, where the pose, lighting and viewpoint can be carefully planned. In this instance, however, the subject is seen in direct sunlight which produces sharp contrasts and saturated colour.

A good portrait will reveal something of the personality of the subject. The face of our elderly Indian market trader, for instance, is deeply furrowed and bears the imprint of a hard-working life. His expression betrays a stoicism and an amused perplexity that anyone should want to paint his portrait!

Artist • Robert Williams

CADMIUM YELLOW BURNT UMBER RAW SIENNA MID-GREY MID-GREEN LAMP BLACK

❶ *An underdrawing is produced on primed hardboard using a No. 6 flat hog's hair brush and Lamp Black.*

❷ *The drawing is further developed in terms of strongly contrasting areas of tone.*

❸ *The turban is painted with Cadmium Yellow and a green-grey is added to the shirt.*

❹ *The background is blocked in with a pale ochre. A mid-brown mixed from Burnt Umber, Raw Sienna and Flake White is painted over the face and while still wet, paler tones of the same colour are used as highlights on the fore-head, nose and cheekbone. The shape of the beard is defined as a dark grey.*

❺ *The texture of the beard is accentuated by using alternate strokes of white and grey. Everything in the final stage is resolved in terms of modelling and tonal values.*

Artist • Sophie Mason

1 *The main outlines of the portrait are drawn in oil pastel onto a primed board.*

2 *Glazes of Cadmium Yellow, Vermilion and crimson are overlaid on the turban, face and background. A neutral grey glaze is painted on the shirt using a broad one-stroke brush.*

3 *Details are broadly established with a thin glaze of Raw Umber. Additionally, the artist indicates where light and shade fall on the head to suggest the modelling of the face.*

CADMIUM YELLOW   VERMILION   CRIMSON   COOL GREY   RAW UMBER   BURNT UMBER

4 *Tones are further modulated generally, using thin broad strokes of grey on the beard and shirt, Burnt Umber and crimson on the face and darker chrome on the turban.*

5 *Sharper tonal contrasts are established overall. Brushstrokes are still very free at this stage.*

6 *Smaller sable brushes are now used to bring greater definition and detail to the painting and to add highlights.*

Artist • John Armstrong

136

① *The primed board is stained with Raw Sienna and allowed to dry. The main proportions are marked in brown using a No. 4 sable brush.*

② *The face is glazed with Burnt Sienna using a hog's hair brush. The shape of the turban is blocked in with Yellow Ochre.*

③ *The folds in the turban are painted in brown. Darker tones are added to the face and a warmer tone painted over the background. The shirt is painted a neutral colour mixed from Terre Verte, brown, Yellow Ochre and white.*

RAW SIENNA   BURNT SIENNA   YELLOW OCHRE   TERRE VERTE   WARM GREY

4 *The modelling of tones on the face is continued using warm greys.*

5 *Lighter tones are painted on the face and more work done on the turban, using a fine sable brush.*

6 *Highlights are added to the turban and warmer whites to the nose and beard.*

Portrait • *Critique*

ROBERT The artist here demonstrates his ability to deal with the intensity of light. Looking at this painting, one has the real sense of the extremities of the climate of India which produces sharp contrasts and purity of colour.

confident handling of intensity of light

skilful handling of colour values

SOPHIE In this painting the artist has somehow managed to get close to the subject so that right away one is riveted by the immediacy and character of the man. Additionally, one is not distracted by any extraneous detail, and colour values are handled skilfully.

Folds in
the cloth of
the turban
are convincing

Could be more
tonal contrast
between
subject and
background

JOHN My attention was first of all directed to the way that the artist has resolved the drawing of the turban! The folds and intertwining of the cloth has been considered and made plausible. The expression on the face of a kind of tranquil sadness has been conveyed equally well. My only reservation is that there could have been more tonal contrast between the subject and his background.

Glossary

A

AERIAL PERSPECTIVE
Sometimes known as atmospheric perspective. Creates the illusion of depth and recession by changes in colour and tone as opposed to measurement.

ALLA PRIMA
The technique by which opaque paint is applied in a single layer to complete the painting in one session.

B

BINDER
The oil that gives cohesion to the pigment – enabling it to adhere to different surfaces.

BLOOM
A white or blue discoloration which can sometimes appear on the surface of a painting – most often when varnished.

BODY
Refers to the actual density of the pigment and its capacity in terms of coverage.

C

CHIAROSCURO
From the Italian, 'light-dark', and refers to the degree of light and dark shading in painting.

COLD (OF COLOUR)
All colours can be related to sensations of warmth or cold. Warm colours tend towards yellows, cold towards blues.

COMPLEMENTARY COLOURS
Complementary colours are found opposite each other on the colour wheel. A colour is complementary to the colour with which it contrasts most strongly, such as red with green.

COMPOSITION
The satisfactory disposition of all elements in a painting.

COPAL
A resin used in the manufacture of varnish.

D

DRY BRUSH
A technique in which the undiluted pigment is skimmed lightly over the surface of a painting leaving a broken effect on the grain of the canvas.

F

FERRULE
The metal part of the brush which binds the hair to the wooden handle.

FILBERT
A brush with bristles forming a flat, tapering shape.

FORM
A term which refers to the three-dimensional appearance of a shape.

FUGITIVE
Used to describe colours that are liable to fade in the course of time.

G

GESSO
A priming agent for canvas and boards made from gypsum.

GLAZE
To modify the painting by applying one transparent film of colour over another.

GROUND
The ground coat of paint which makes a surface suitable for painting on. Can also be the first colour laid on the surface as a base tone.

H

HALFTONE
A tone mid-way between black and white, or the strength between the lightest and darkest tone.

HUE
The colour, rather than the tone, of a pigment or object.

I

IMPASTO
A heavy paste-like application of paint which produces a textured effect.

L

LOCAL COLOUR
The actual colour of an object, such as the red of an apple, rather than a colour which is modified by light or shade.

M

MEDIUM

The medium is (a) the type of material used to produce a drawing or painting e.g. charcoal, pastel, watercolour, oil etc., or (b) a substance blended with paint to thicken, thin or dry the paint.

MODELLING

Expressing the volume and solidity of an object by light and shade.

MONOCHROME

Refers to a painting produced with a single colour, gradations of colour, or in black and white.

MULLER

A heavy slab of marble with curved edges used for grinding coloured pigment.

 P

PALETTE

This can be (a) the surface on which the colours are mixed, or (b) a particular range of colours selected individually by the artist.

PIGMENT

The coloured matter of paint originally derived from plants, animal, vegetable and mineral products. Generally synthesised chemically in paint manufacture.

 S

SCUMBLING

A technique whereby an opaque colour is dragged roughly across another, producing a broken texture.

SUPPORT

The surface on which a painting is made (canvas, wood, hardboard etc.).

 T

TONE

The light and dark value of a colour; for example, pale red is the same tone as pale ochre but both are lighter in tone than dark brown.

 U

UNDERPAINTING

The first laying-in of the underlying drawing in thin transparent paint.

W

WET-IN-WET

A technique which allows colours to merge randomly whilst still wet.

Index

Index